THE WORKS OF
EUGENE FIELD

Vol. III

TELLING THE BEES

THE WRITINGS IN PROSE AND VERSE OF EUGENE FIELD

SECOND BOOK OF VERSE ❧

CHARLES SCRIBNER'S SONS ❧ NEW YORK ❧ 1896

A LITTLE bit of a woman came
    Athwart my path one day;
So tiny was she that she seemed to be
A pixy strayed from the misty sea,
    Or a wandering greenwood fay.

"Oho, you little elf!" I cried,
    "And what are you doing here?
So tiny as you will never do
For the brutal rush and hullaballoo
    Of this practical world, I fear."

"Voice have I, good sir," said she. —
    "'T is soft as an Angel's sigh,
But to fancy a word of yours were heard
In all the din of this world's absurd!"
    Smiling, I made reply.

"Hands have I, good sir," she quoth. —
    "Marry, and that have you!
But amid the strife and the tumult rife
In all the struggle and battle for life,
    What can those wee hands do?"

v

"Eyes have I, good sir," she said. —
  "Sooth, you have," quoth I,
"And tears shall flow therefrom, I trow,
  And they betimes shall dim with woe,
    As the hard, hard years go by!"

That little bit of a woman cast
  Her two eyes full on me,
And they smote me sore to my inmost core,
And they hold me slaved forevermore, —
  Yet would I not be free!

That little bit of a woman's hands
  Reached up into my breast,
And rent apart my scoffing heart, —
And they buffet it still with such sweet art
  As cannot be expressed.

That little bit of a woman's voice
  Hath grown most wondrous dear ;
Above the blare of all elsewhere
(An inspiration that mocks at care)
  It riseth full and clear.

Dear one, I bless the subtle power
  That makes me wholly thine ;
And I 'm proud to say that I bless the day
When a little woman wrought her way
  Into this life of mine!

INTRODUCTION

EUGENE FIELD

A HOMESPUN, homely, humorous, tender man is dear to human nature; and when such a man is brightened by genius he becomes inestimable. We find in him both heaven and earth — our aspirations and ourselves; and simply by living with us he makes us happier and better men. Of the American breed of such benefactors, Abraham Lincoln is the largest and completest type. His destiny was the mightiest that can fall to a man, and his achievement matched it: but we love him even more than we admire and wonder at him, because the humblest of us find in him so much that belongs to us. We have part in his aims, in his difficulties, and in his victories, by dint of the spontaneous sympathy he awakens in us. And the same qualities in kind that make the world love Lincoln, make all who knew Field love him.

But his death is too recent for me to have attained a mood in which to make a cool and balanced analysis of him. It will always be so. I miss him more since the lapse of these few months than I did at the first shock of the news that he was gone. We bury little losses; but the great ones become a sort of dwelling-place for the memory, and our continual resort. There is nothing morbid or barren there. When I think of my friend, all the hours that we spent and the words that we spoke together re-create him in my mind and heart, till I hear his very voice and see his face again. While he still lived among us, these memories were less vivid, because I hoped to see him soon once more, and slighted the past in anticipation of the future. But now that the past is all I have, I value it as does the shipwrecked sailor the fragments of his vessel, from which he must build a raft to bear him to the untravelled seas.

He was the most cheerful and wholesome of companions; because, though he must have endured his full share of human anxieties and responsibilities, yet he regarded himself so little, and others so much, that he was constantly out-of-doors as it were, in the fresh air and sunshine of charity and sympathy. He would not brood over his troubles, but learned from them how to lighten the troubles of his friends. His sense of humor, too, was of the deeper sort that perceives the eternal law underlying the passing phenomenon, and smiles at the apparent incongruity. Glancing up from the accidents of the street to the immutability of the stars, he found both fun and pathos in the turmoil of those who would limit the play of human destiny to the former. You could not frighten him with worldly misfortunes, because he was a citizen of the universe; and I suspect he may have loved Chicago for its littleness quite as much as for its greatness. He criticised his fellow-townspeople faithfully and stringently to the last, while never even in thought setting himself a hair's breath higher than the humblest of them.

So warm and wide a mind as his could not

but be creative, and he was observant enough to give his creations distinctness as well as distinction. But a lovely fancy, rising ever and anon to the imaginative height, was perhaps his predominant literary trait. Left to himself, his footsteps always tended towards Fairy Land; and the quaint Gothic bias in him led him to delight in mediæval idioms and orthography. "Madge the Hoyden" could not have been expressed in contemporary English, though her life and fate appeal to the heart of all ages. Field used to tell me that he could not imagine himself writing a "modern" novel : nor, upon reflection, could I. He loved the illuminated missals of the old monks, their black-letter, their massy bindings and clasps, their gargoyles and hobgoblins, and all the mystic extravagance of chivalry. This rich old atmosphere stimulated and pleased him, till you might have thought he had strayed down to us from the Fourteenth Century, with all its habitudes about him. But then, what queer freak of fate was it that conducted this wandering monk or minstrel to a newspaper-office in the most modern of cities, and set him to inditing paragraphs of quips and conceits on the doings of to-day and to-morrow? What might not he have accomplished, who did even this so well?

His domestic life, however, was probably the most important factor in his career, as it undoubtedly was in his happiness. How he loved his home folk, and they him! And in his poems and tales you see paramount the sweet and gentle influence of wife, mother, and children. Nothing so nearly perfect in child-literature has ever been written as are many of these exquisite verses of Field. In writing them, he is at once child and poet, son and mother, wife and husband. And what shall we say of his translations of Horace, except that many of them are unsurpassably good? Wide indeed were the scope and orbit of his intelligence and sympathy!

And therefore all that I have here written is inadequate and vain: he was not what I have said, because he was so much more. I cannot compass him. "There's poverty in the love that can be reckoned," and it is partly because he was personally so much to me that I cannot picture him to others.

The world is better for his brief participation in its fortunes; and the departure of such a man as he must awaken and fix the heavenward hopes of all who knew his manhood, faith, and aim.

JULIAN HAWTHORNE.

The Verse in this Second Book

CONTENTS

CONTENTS

xv

Second Book of Verse.

FATHER'S WAY

Y father was no pessimist; he loved
the things of earth,—
Its cheerfulness and sunshine, its
music and its mirth.
He never sighed or moped around whenever
things went wrong,—
I warrant me he'd mocked at fate with some
defiant song;
But, being he war n't much on tune, when
times looked sort o' blue,
He'd whistle softly to himself this only tune
he knew,—

Now mother, when she heard that tune
    which father whistled so,
Would say, "There's something wrong to-
    day with Ephraim, I know;
He never tries to make believe he's happy
    that 'ere way
But that I'm certain as can be there's some-
    thin' wrong to pay."
And so betimes, quite natural-like, to us ob-
    servant youth
There seemed suggestion in that tune of
    deep, pathetic truth.

When Brother William joined the war, a lot
    of us went down
To see the gallant soldier boys right gayly
    out of town.
A-comin' home, poor mother cried as if her
    heart would break,
And all us children, too,—for *hers*, and *not*
    for *William's* sake!
But father, trudgin' on ahead, his hands be-
    hind him so,
Kept whistlin' to himself, so sort of solemn-
    like and low.

And when my oldest sister, Sue, was married
    and went West,
Seemed like it took the tuck right out of
    mother and the rest.
She was the sunlight in our home, — why,
    father used to say
It would n't seem like home at all if Sue
    should go away;
But when she went, a-leavin' us all sorrer
    and all tears,
Poor father whistled lonesome-like — and
    went to feed the steers.

When crops were bad, and other ills befell
    our homely lot,
He 'd set of nights and try to act as if he
    minded not;
And when came death and bore away the
    one he worshipped so,
How vainly did his lips belie the heart be-
    numbed with woe!
You see the telltale whistle told a mood
    he 'd not admit, —
He 'd always stopped his whistlin' when he
    thought we noticed it.

I'd like to see that stooping form and hoary
    head again,—
To see the honest, hearty smile that cheered
    his fellow-men.
Oh, could I kiss the kindly lips that spake
    no creature wrong,
And share the rapture of the heart that over-
    flowed with song!
Oh, could I hear the little tune he whistled
    long ago,
When he did battle with the griefs he would
    not have *us* know!

TO MY MOTHER

HOW fair you are, my mother!
    Ah, though 't is many a year
    Since you were here,
Still do I see your beauteous face,
    And with the glow
Of your dark eyes cometh a grace
    Of long ago.
So gentle, too, my mother!
    Just as of old, upon my brow,
    Like benedictions now,
Falleth your dear hand's touch;
    And still, as then,
A voice that glads me over-much
    Cometh again,
    My fair and gentle mother!

How you have loved me, mother,
    I have not power to tell,
    Knowing full well

5

That even in the rest above
   It is your will
To watch and guard me with your love,
   Loving me still.
And, as of old, my mother,
   I am content to be a child,
   By mother's love beguiled
From all these other charms;
   So to the last
Within thy dear, protecting arms
   Hold thou me fast,
   My guardian angel, mother!

KÖRNER'S BATTLE PRAYER

FATHER, I cry to Thee!
  Round me the billows of battle
    are pouring,
Round me the thunders of battle are roar-
    ing;
  Father on high, hear Thou my cry,—
  Father, oh, lead Thou me!

Father, oh, lead Thou me!
Lead me, o'er Death and its terrors victo-
    rious,—
See, I acknowledge Thy will as all-glorious;
  Point thou the way, lead where it may,—
  God, I acknowledge Thee!

7

God, I acknowledge Thee!
As when the dead leaves of autumn whirl
    round me,
So, when the horrors of war would con-
    found me,
    Laugh I at fear, knowing Thee near,—
    Father, oh, bless Thou me!

Father, oh, bless Thou me!
Living or dying, waking or sleeping,
Such as I am, I commit to Thy keeping:
    Frail though I be, Lord, bless Thou me!
    Father, I worship Thee!

Father, I worship Thee!
Not for the love of the riches that perish,
But for the freedom and justice we cherish,
    Stand we or fall, blessing Thee, all—
    God, I submit to Thee!

God, I submit to Thee!
Yea, though the terrors of Death pass before
    me,
Yea, with the darkness of Death stealing
    o'er me,
    Lord, unto Thee bend I the knee,—
    Father, I cry to Thee!

GOSLING STEW

IN Oberhausen, on a time,
   I fared as might a king;
And now I feel the muse sublime
Inspire me to embalm in rhyme
   That succulent and sapid thing
Behight of gentile and of Jew
      A gosling stew!

The good Herr Schmitz brought out his
    best,—
   Soup, cutlet, salad, roast,—
And I partook with hearty zest,
And fervently anon I blessed
   That generous and benignant host,
When suddenly dawned on my view
      A gosling stew!

9

I sniffed it coming on apace,
   And as its odors filled
The curious little dining-place,
I felt a glow suffuse my face,
   I felt my very marrow thrilled
With rapture altogether new,—
      'T was gosling stew!

These callow birds had never played
   In yonder village pond;
Had never through the gateway strayed,
And plaintive spissant music made
   Upon the grassy green beyond:
Cooped up, they simply ate and grew
      For gosling stew!

My doctor said I must n't eat
   High food and seasoned game;
But surely gosling is a meat
With tender nourishment replete.
   Leastwise I gayly ate this same;
I braved dyspepsy — would n't you
      For gosling stew?

I 've feasted where the possums grow,
   Roast turkey have I tried,
The joys of canvasbacks I know,
And frequently I 've eaten crow
   In bleak and chill Novembertide;
I 'd barter all that native crew
     For gosling stew!

And when from Rhineland I adjourn
   To seek my Yankee shore,
Back shall my memory often turn,
And fiercely shall my palate burn
   For sweets I 'll taste, alas! no more,—
Oh, that mein kleine frau could brew
     A gosling stew!

Vain are these keen regrets of mine,
   And vain the song I sing;
Yet would I quaff a stoup of wine
To Oberhausen auf der Rhine,
   Where fared I like a very king:
And here 's a last and fond adieu
     To gosling stew!

CATULLUS TO LESBIA

COME, my Lesbia, no repining;
     Let us love while yet we may!
Suns go on forever shining;
     But when we have had our day,
Sleep perpetual shall o'ertake us,
And no morrow's dawn awake us.

Come, in yonder nook reclining,
     Where the honeysuckle climbs,
Let us mock at Fate's designing,
     Let us kiss a thousand times!
And if they shall prove too few, dear,
When they 're kissed we 'll start anew, dear!

And should any chance to see us,
     Goodness! how they 'll agonize!
How they 'll wish that they could be us,
     Kissing in such liberal wise!
Never mind their envious whining;
Come, my Lesbia, no repining!

JOHN SMITH

TO-DAY I strayed in Charing Cross, as
    wretched as could be,
With thinking of my home and friends across
    the tumbling sea;
There was no water in my eyes, but my
    spirits were depressed,
And my heart lay like a sodden, soggy
    doughnut in my breast.
This way and that streamed multitudes, that
    gayly passed me by;
Not one in all the crowd knew me, and not
    a one knew I.
"Oh for a touch of home!" I sighed; "oh
    for a friendly face!
Oh for a hearty hand-clasp in this teeming,
    desert place!"
And so soliloquizing, as a homesick creature
    will,
Incontinent, I wandered down the noisy,
    bustling hill,

And drifted, automatic-like and vaguely, into
    Lowe's,
Where Fortune had in store a panacea for
    my woes.
The register was open, and there dawned
    upon my sight
A name that filled and thrilled me with a
    cyclone of delight,—
The name that I shall venerate unto my
    dying day,
The proud, immortal signature: "John
    Smith, U. S. A."

Wildly I clutched the register, and brooded
    on that name;
I knew John Smith, yet could not well iden-
    tify the same.
I knew him North, I knew him South, I
    knew him East and West:
I knew him all so well I knew not which I
    knew the best.
His eyes, I recollect, were gray, and black,
    and brown, and blue;
And when he was not bald, his hair was of
    chameleon hue;

Lean, fat, tall, short, rich, poor, grave, gay,
  a blonde and a brunette,—
Aha, amid this London fog, John Smith, I
  see you yet!
I see you yet; and yet the sight is all so
  blurred I seem
To see you in composite, or as in a waking
  dream.
Which are you, John? I 'd like to know,
  that I might weave a rhyme
Appropriate to your character, your politics,
  and clime.
So tell me, were you "raised" or "reared"?
  your pedigree confess
In some such treacherous ism as "I reckon"
  or "I guess."
Let fall your telltale dialect, that instantly I
  may
Identify my countryman, "John Smith, U.
  S. A."
It 's like as not you air the John that lived a
  spell ago
Deown East, where codfish, beans, 'nd *bona-
  fide* schoolma'ams grow;
Where the dear old homestead nestles like
  among the Hampshire hills,

15

And where the robin hops about the cherry-
    boughs, 'nd trills;
Where Hubbard squash 'nd huckleberries
    grow to powerful size,
And everything is orthodox from preachers
    down to pies;
Where the red-wing blackbirds swing 'nd
    call beside the pick'ril pond,
And the crows air cawin' in the pines uv
    the pasture lot beyond;
Where folks complain uv bein' poor, because
    their money's lent
Out West on farms 'nd railroads at the rate
    uv ten per cent;
Where we ust to spark the Baker girls a-
    comin' home from choir,
Or a-settin' namin' apples round the roarin'
    kitchen fire;
Where we had to go to meetin' at least three
    times a week,
And our mothers learnt us good religious
    Dr. Watts to speak;
And where our grandmas sleep their sleep —
    God rest their souls, I say;
And God bless yours, ef you 're that John,
    "John Smith, U. S. A."

Or, mebbe, Col. Smith, yo' are the gentle-
man I know

In the country whar the finest Democrats
'nd hosses grow;

Whar the ladies are all beautiful, an' whar
the crap of cawn

Is utilized for Burbon, and true awters are
bawn.

You 've ren for jedge, and killed yore man,
and bet on Proctor Knott;

Yore heart is full of chivalry, yore skin is
full of shot;

And I disremember whar I 've met with
gentlemen so true

As yo' all in Kaintucky, whar blood an' grass
are blue,

Whar a niggah with a ballot is the signal fo'
a fight,

Whar the yaller dawg pursues the coon
throughout the bammy night,

Whar blooms the furtive possum,— pride
an' glory of the South!

And anty makes a hoe-cake, sah, that melts
within yo' mouth,

Whar all night long the mockin'-birds are
warblin' in the trees,

17

And black-eyed Susans nod and blink at
    every passing breeze,
Whar in a hallowed soil repose the ashes of
    our Clay,—
H'yar 's lookin' at yo', Col. "John Smith,
    U. S. A."

Or wuz you that John Smith I knew out
    yonder in the West,—
That part of our Republic I shall always love
    the best!
Wuz you him that went prospectin' in the
    spring of '69
In the Red Hoss Mountain country for the
    Gosh-all-Hemlock mine?
Oh, how I 'd liked to clasped your hand, an'
    set down by your side,
And talked about the good old days beyond
    the Big Divide,—
Of the rackaboar, the snaix, the bear, the
    Rocky Mountain goat,
Of the conversazzhyony, 'nd of Casey's tab-
    ble dote,
And a word of them old pardners that stood
    by us long ago,—

Three-fingered Hoover, Sorry Tom, and Parson Jim, you know!
Old times, old friends, John Smith, would make our hearts beat high again,
And we 'd see the snow-top mountains like we used to see 'em then;
The magpies would go flutterin' like strange sperrits to 'nd fro,
And we 'd hear the pines a-singin' in the ragged gulch below;
And the mountain brook would loiter like upon its windin' way,
Ez if it waited for a child to jine it in its play.
You see, John Smith, just which you are I cannot well recall;
And, really, I am pleased to think you somehow must be all!
For when a man sojourns abroad awhile, as I have done,
He likes to think of all the folks he left at home as one.
And so they are,— for well you know there 's nothing in a name;
Our Browns, our Joneses, and our Smiths are happily the same,—

19

All represent the spirit of the land across the
    sea;
All stand for one high purpose in our country
    of the free.
Whether John Smith be from the South, the
    North, the West, the East,
So long as he 's American, it mattereth not
    the least;
Whether his crest be badger, bear, palmetto,
    sword, or pine,
His is the glory of the stars that with the
    stripes combine.
Where'er he be, whate'er his lot, he 's eager
    to be known,
Not by his mortal name, but by his country's
    name alone;
And so, compatriot, I am proud you wrote
    your name to-day
Upon the register at Lowe's, "John Smith,
    U. S. A."

ST. MARTIN'S LANE

ST. MARTIN'S LANE winds up the hill
And trends a devious way;
I walk therein amid the din
Of busy London day:
I walk where wealth and squalor meet,
And think upon a time
When others trod this saintly sod,
And heard St. Martin's chime.

But when those solemn bells invoke
The midnight's slumbrous grace,
The ghosts of men come back again
To haunt that curious place:
The ghosts of sages, poets, wits,
Come back in goodly train;
And all night long, with mirth and song,
They walk St. Martin's Lane.

There 's Jerrold paired with Thackeray,
    Maginn and Thomas Moore,
And here and there and everywhere
    Fraserians by the score;
And one wee ghost that climbs the hill
    Is welcomed with a shout,—
No king could be revered as he,—
    The *padre,* Father Prout!

They banter up and down the street,
    And clamor at the door
Of yonder inn, which once has been
    The scene of mirth galore:
'T is now a lonely, musty shell,
    Deserted, like to fall;
And Echo mocks their ghostly knocks,
    And iterates their call.

Come back, thou ghost of ruddy host,
    From Pluto's misty shore;
Renew to-night the keen delight
    Of by-gone years once more;
Brew for this merry, motley horde,
    And serve the steaming cheer;
And grant that I may lurk hard by,
    To see the mirth, and hear.

Ah, me! I dream what things may seem
  To others childish vain,
And yet at night 't is my delight
  To walk St. Martin's Lane;
For, in the light of other days,
  I walk with those I love,
And all the time St. Martin's chime
  Makes piteous moan above.

DEAR OLD LONDON

WHEN I was broke in London in the
  fall of '89,
I chanced to spy in Oxford Street this tanta-
  lizing sign,—
" A Splendid Horace cheap for Cash!" Of
  course I had to look
Upon the vaunted bargain, and it was a
  noble book!
A finer one I 've never seen, nor can I hope
  to see,—
The first edition, richly bound, and clean as
  clean can be;
And, just to think, for three-pounds-ten I
  might have had that Pine,
When I was broke in London in the fall of
  '89!

24

Down at Noseda's, in the Strand, I found,
    one fateful day,
A portrait that I pined for as only maniac
    may,—
A print of Madame Vestris (she flourished
    years ago,
Was Bartolozzi's daughter and a thorough-
    bred, you know).
A clean and handsome print it was, and
    cheap at thirty bob,—
That 's what I told the salesman, as I choked
    a rising sob;
But I hung around Noseda's as it were a
    holy shrine,
When I was broke in London in the fall of
    '89.

At Davey's, in Great Russell Street, were
    autographs galore,
And Mr. Davey used to let me con that pre-
    cious store.
Sometimes I read what warriors wrote,
    sometimes a king's command,
But oftener still a poet's verse, writ in a
    meagre hand.

25

Lamb, Byron, Addison, and Burns, Pope,
    Johnson, Swift, and Scott,—
It needed but a paltry sum to comprehend
    the lot;
Yet, though Friend Davey marked 'em down,
    what could I but decline ?
For I was broke in London in the fall of '89.

Of antique swords and spears I saw a vast
    and dazzling heap
That Curio Fenton offered me at prices pass-
    ing cheap;
And, oh, the quaint old bureaus, and the
    warming-pans of brass,
And the lovely hideous freaks I found in
    pewter and in glass!
And, oh, the sideboards, candlesticks, the
    cracked old china plates,
The clocks and spoons from Amsterdam
    that antedate all dates!
Of such superb monstrosities I found an
    endless mine
When I was broke in London in the fall of
    '89.

26

O ye that hanker after boons that others idle
    by,—
The battered things that please the soul,
    though they may vex the eye,—
The silver plate and crockery all sanctified
    with grime,
The oaken stuff that has defied the tooth of
    envious Time,
The musty tomes, the speckled prints, the
    mildewed bills of play,
And other costly relics of malodorous
    decay,—
Ye only can appreciate what agony was
    mine
When I was broke in London in the fall
    of '89.

When, in the course of natural things, I go
    to my reward,
Let no imposing epitaph my martyrdoms
    record;
Neither in Hebrew, Latin, Greek, nor any
    classic tongue,
Let my ten thousand triumphs over human
    griefs be sung;

But in plain Anglo-Saxon — that he may
    know who seeks
What agonizing pangs I 've had while on
    the hunt for freaks —
Let there be writ upon the slab that marks
    my grave this line:
" Deceased was broke in London in the fall
    of '89."

CORSICAN LULLABY

BAMBINO in his cradle slept;
    And by his side his grandam grim
Bent down and smiled upon the child,
    And sung this lullaby to him,—
        This "ninna and anninia":

"When thou art older, thou shalt mind
    To traverse countries far and wide,
And thou shalt go where roses blow
    And balmy waters singing glide —
        So ninna and anninia!

"And thou shalt wear, trimmed up in points,
    A famous jacket edged in red,
And, more than that, a peakèd hat,
    All decked in gold, upon thy head —
        Ah! ninna and anninia!

29

"Then shalt thou carry gun and knife,
  Nor shall the soldiers bully thee;
Perchance, beset by wrong or debt,
  A mighty bandit thou shalt be —
    So ninna and anninia!

"No woman yet of our proud race
  Lived to her fourteenth year unwed;
The brazen churl that eyed a girl
  Bought her the ring or paid his head —
    So ninna and anninia!

"But once came spies (I know the thieves!)
  And brought disaster to our race;
God heard us when our fifteen men
  Were hanged within the market-place —
    But ninna and anninia!

"Good men they were, my babe, and true, —
  Right worthy fellows all, and strong;
Live thou and be for them and me
  Avenger of that deadly wrong —
    So ninna and anninia!"

THE CLINK OF THE ICE

NOTABLY fond of music, I dote on a
    sweeter tone
Than ever the harp has uttered or ever the
    lute has known.
When I wake at five in the morning with a
    feeling in my head
Suggestive of mild excesses before I retired
    to bed;
When a small but fierce volcano vexes me
    sore inside,
And my throat and mouth are furred with a
    fur that seemeth a buffalo hide,—
How gracious those dews of solace that over
    my senses fall
At the clink of the ice in the pitcher the boy
    brings up the hall!
Oh, is it the gaudy ballet, with features I
    cannot name,
That kindles in virile bosoms that slow but
    devouring flame?

Or is it the midnight supper, eaten before
    we retire,
That presently by combustion setteth us all
    afire ?
Or is it the cheery magnum ? — nay, I 'll not
    chide the cup
That makes the meekest mortal anxious to
    whoop things up:
Yet, what the cause soever, relief comes
    when we call, —
Relief with that rapturous clinkety-clink that
    clinketh alike for all.

I 've dreamt of the fiery furnace that was
    one vast bulk of flame,
And that I was Abednego a-wallowing in
    that same;
And I 've dreamt I was a crater, possessed
    of a mad desire
To vomit molten lava, and to snort big gobs
    of fire;
I 've dreamt I was Roman candles and rock-
    ets that fizzed and screamed, —
In short, I have dreamt the cussedest dreams
    that ever a human dreamed:

But all the red-hot fancies were scattered
    quick as a wink
When the spirit within that pitcher went
    clinking its clinkety-clink.

Boy, why so slow in coming with that gra-
    cious, saving cup?
Oh, haste thee to the succor of the man who
    is burning up!
See how the ice bobs up and down, as if it
    wildly strove
To reach its grace to the wretch who feels
    like a red-hot kitchen stove!
The piteous clinks it clinks methinks should
    thrill you through and through:
An erring soul is wanting drink, and he
    wants it p. d. q.!
And, lo! the honest pitcher, too, falls in so
    dire a fret
That its pallid form is presently bedewed
    with a chilly sweat.

May blessings be showered upon the man
    who first devised this drink
That happens along at five A. M. with its rap-
    turous clinkety-clink!

I never have felt the cooling flood go sizzling
    down my throat
But what I vowed to hymn a hymn to that
    clinkety-clink devote;
So now, in the prime of my manhood, I pol-
    ish this lyric gem
For the uses of all good fellows who are
    thirsty at five A. M.,
But specially for those fellows who have
    known the pleasing thrall
Of the clink of the ice in the pitcher the boy
    brings up the hall.

THE BELLS OF NOTRE DAME

WHAT though the radiant thoroughfare
   Teems with a noisy throng?
What though men bandy everywhere
  The ribald jest and song?"
Over the din of oaths and cries
  Broodeth a wondrous calm,
And 'mid that solemn stillness rise
  The bells of Notre Dame.

"Heed not, dear Lord," they seem to say,
  "Thy weak and erring child;
And thou, O gentle Mother, pray
  That God be reconciled;
And on mankind, O Christ, our King,
  Pour out Thy gracious balm,"—
'T is thus they plead and thus they sing,
  Those bells of Notre Dame.

And so, methinks, God, bending down
   To ken the things of earth,
Heeds not the mockery of the town
   Or cries of ribald mirth;
For ever soundeth in His ears
   A penitential psalm,—
'T is thy angelic voice He hears,
   O bells of Notre Dame!

Plead on, O bells, that thy sweet voice
   May still forever be
An intercession to rejoice
   Benign divinity;
And that thy tuneful grace may fall
   Like dew, a quickening balm,
Upon the arid hearts of all,
   O bells of Notre Dame!

LOVER'S LANE, SAINT JO

SAINT JO, Buchanan County,
  Is leagues and leagues away;
And I sit in the gloom of this rented room,
  And pine to be there to-day.
Yes, with London fog around me
  And the bustling to and fro,
I am fretting to be across the sea
  In Lover's Lane, Saint Jo.

I would have a brown-eyed maiden
  Go driving once again;
And I 'd sing the song, as we snailed along,
  That I sung to that maiden then:
I purposely say, "as we *snailed* along,"
  For a proper horse goes slow
In those leafy aisles, where Cupid smiles,
  In Lover's Lane, Saint Jo.

From her boudoir in the alders
    Would peep a lynx-eyed thrush,
And we 'd hear her say, in a furtive way,
    To the noisy cricket, "Hush!"
To think that the curious creature
    Should crane her neck to know
The various things one says and sings
    In Lover's Lane, Saint Jo.

But the maples they should shield us
    From the gossips of the place;
Nor should the sun, except by pun,
    Profane the maiden's face;
And the girl should do the driving,
    For a fellow can't, you know,
Unless he 's neglectful of what 's quite re-
      spectful
    In Lover's Lane, Saint Jo.

Ah! sweet the hours of springtime,
    When the heart inclines to woo,
And it 's deemed all right for the callow
      wight
    To do what he wants to do;

But cruel the age of winter,
    When the way of the world says no
To the hoary men who would woo again
    In Lover's Lane, Saint Jo!

In the Union Bank of London
    Are forty pounds or more,
Which I 'm like to spend, ere the month
      shall end,
    In an antiquarian store;
But I 'd give it all, and gladly,
    If for an hour or so
I could feel the grace of a distant place,—
    Of Lover's Lane, Saint Jo.

Let us sit awhile, beloved,
    And dream of the good old days,—
Of the kindly shade which the maples made
    Round the stanch but squeaky chaise;
With your head upon my shoulder,
    And my arm about you so,
Though exiles, we shall seem to be
    In Lover's Lane, Saint Jo.

CRUMPETS AND TEA

THERE are happenings in life that are
    destined to rise
Like dear, hallowed visions before a man's
    eyes;
And the passage of years shall not dim in
    the least
The glory and joy of our Sabbath-day feast,—
The Sabbath-day luncheon that 's spread for
    us three,—
My worthy companions, Teresa and Leigh,
And me, all so hungry for crumpets and tea.

There are cynics who say with invidious zest
That a crumpet 's a thing that will never
    digest;
But I happen to *know* that a crumpet is
    prime
For digestion, if only you give it its time.

Or if, by a chance, it should *not* quite agree,
Why, who would begrudge a physician his fee
For plying his trade upon crumpets and tea?

To toast crumpets quite *à la mode*, I require
A proper long fork and a proper quick fire;
And when they are browned, without further
    ado,
I put on the butter, that soaks through and
    through.
And meantime Teresa, directed by Leigh,
Compounds and pours out a rich brew for
    us three;
And so we sit down to our crumpets — and
    tea.

A hand-organ grinds in the street a weird
    bit,—
Confound those Italians! I wish they would
    quit
Interrupting our feast with their dolorous airs,
Suggestive of climbing the heavenly stairs.
(It 's thoughts of the future, as all will agree,
That we fain would dismiss from our bosoms
    when we
Sit down to discussion of crumpets and tea!)

The Sabbath-day luncheon whereof I now
    speak
Quite answers its purpose the rest of the
    week;
Yet with the next Sabbath I wait for the bell
Announcing the man who has crumpets to
    sell;
Then I scuttle downstairs in a frenzy of glee,
And purchase for sixpence enough for us
    three,
Who hunger and hanker for crumpets and
    tea.

But soon—ah! too soon—I must bid a fare-
    well
To joys that succeed to the sound of that
    bell,
Must hie me away from the dank, foggy
    shore
That 's filled me with colic and—yearnings
    for more!
Then the cruel, the heartless, the conscience-
    less sea
Shall bear me afar from Teresa and Leigh
And the other twin friendships of crumpets
    and tea.

Yet often, ay, ever, before my wan eyes
That Sabbath-day luncheon of old shall arise.
My stomach, perhaps, shall improve by the
    change,
Since crumpets it seems to prefer at long
    range;
But, oh, how my palate will hanker to be
In London again with Teresa and Leigh,
Enjoying the rapture of crumpets and tea!

AN IMITATION OF DR. WATTS

THROUGH all my life the poor shall find
　　In me a constant friend;
And on the meek of every kind
　　My mercy shall attend.

The dumb shall never call on me
　　In vain for kindly aid;
And in my hands the blind shall see
　　A bounteous alms displayed.

In all their walks the lame shall know
　　And feel my goodness near;
And on the deaf will I bestow
　　My gentlest words of cheer.

'T is by such pious works as these,
　　Which I delight to do,
That men their fellow-creatures please,
　　And please their Maker too.

44

MODJESKY AS CAMEEL

A FORE we went to Denver we had heerd
the Tabor Grand,
Allowed by critics ez the finest opry in the
land;
And, roundin' up at Denver in the fall of '81,
Well heeled in p'int uv looker 'nd a-pinin' for
some fun,
We told Bill Bush that we wuz fixed quite
comf'table for wealth,
And had n't struck that altitood entirely for
our health.
You see we knew Bill Bush at Central City
years ago;
(An' a whiter man than that same Bill you
could not wish to know!)
Bill run the Grand for Tabor, 'nd he gin us
two a deal
Ez how we really otter see Modjesky ez
Cameel.

Three-Fingered Hoover stated that he 'd great
    deal ruther go
To call on Charley Simpson than frequent a'
    opry show.
"The queen uv tradegy," sez he, "is wot
    I 've never seen,
And I reckon there is more for *me* in some
    other kind uv queen."
"Git out!" sez Bill, disgusted-like, "and
    can't you never find
A pleasure in the things uv life wich ellervates
    the mind?
You 've set around in Casey's restauraw a
    year or more,
An' heerd ol' Vere de Blaw perform shef
    doovers by the score,
Only to come down here among us *tong* an'
    say you feel
You 'd ruther take in faro than a' opry like
    'Cameel'!"

But it seems it wur n't no opry, but a sort
    uv foreign play,
With a heap uv talk an' dressin' that wuz
    both de*kolly*tay.

A young chap sparks a gal, who's caught a
    dook that's old an' wealthy,—
She has a cold 'nd faintin' fits, and is gin'rally
    onhealthy.
She says she has a record; but the young
    chap does n't mind,
And it looks ez if the feller wuz a proper
    likely kind
Until his old man sneaks around 'nd makes
    a dirty break,
And the young one plays the sucker 'nd gives
    the girl the shake.
"Armo! Armo!" she hollers; but he flings
    her on the floor,
And says he ain'ter goin' to have no truck
    with her no more.

At that Three-Fingered Hoover says, "I 'll
    chip into this game,
And see if Red Hoss Mountain cannot recon-
    struct the same.
I won't set by an' see the feelin's uv a lady
    hurt,—
Gol durn a critter, anyhow, that does a wo-
    man dirt!"

47

He riz up like a giant in that little painted
    pen,
And stepped upon the platform with the
    women-folks 'nd men;
Across the trough of gaslights he bounded
    like a deer,
An' grabbed Armo an' hove him through the
    landscape in the rear;
And then we seen him shed his hat an' rev-
    erently kneel,
An' put his strong arms tenderly around the
    gal Cameel.

A-standin' in his stockin' feet, his height wuz
    six foot three,
And a huskier man than Hoover wuz you
    could not hope to see.
He downed Lafe Dawson wrasslin'; and one
    night I seen him lick
Three Cornish miners that come into camp
    from Roarin' Crick
To clean out Casey's restauraw an' do the
    town, they said.
He could whip his weight in wildcats, an'
    paint whole townships red,

But good to helpless folks and weak,— a
　　brave and manly heart
A cyclone could n't phase, but any child could
　　rend apart;
Jest like the mountain pine, wich dares the
　　storm that howls along,
But rocks the winds uv summer-time, an'
　　sings a soothin' song.

"Cameel," sez he, "your record is ag'in you,
　　I 'll allow,
But, bein' you 're a woman, you 'll git justice
　　anyhow;
So, if you say you 're sorry, and intend to
　　travel straight,—
Why, never mind that other chap with which
　　you meant to mate,—
I 'll marry you myself, and take you back to-
　　morrow night
To the camp on Red Hoss Mountain, where
　　the boys 'll treat you white,
Where Casey runs a tabble dote, and folks are
　　brave 'nd true,
Where there ain't no ancient history to bother
　　me or you,

Where there ain't no law but honesty, no
    evidence but facts,
Where between the verdict and the rope
    there ain't no *onter acts*.''

I wuz mighty proud of Hoover; but the folks
    began to shout
That the feller was intrudin', and would some
    one put him out.
''Well, no; I reckon not,'' says I, or words
    to that effect,
Ez I perduced a' argument I thought they
    might respect,—
A long an' harnsome weepon I'd preëmpted
    when I come
Out West (its cartridges wuz big an' juicy ez
    a plum),
Wich, when persented properly, wuz very
    apt to sway
The popular opinion in a most persuasive
    way.
''Well, no; I reckon not,'' says I; but I
    did n't say no more,
Observin' that there wuz a ginral movement
    towards the door.

First Dr. Lemen he allowed that he had got
    to go
And see a patient he jest heerd wuz lyin'
    very low;
An' Charlie Toll riz up an' said he guessed
    he 'd jine the Dock,
An' go to see a client wich wuz waitin' round
    the block;
John Arkins reckollected he had interviews
    to write,
And previous engagements hurried Cooper
    from our sight;
Cal Cole went out to buy a hoss, Fred Skiff
    and Belford too;
And Stapleton remembered he had heaps uv
    work to do.
Somehow or other every one wuz full uv
    business then;
Leastwise, they all vamoosed, and did n't
    bother us again.

I reckollect that Willard Morse an' Bush come
    runnin' in,
A-hollerin', "Oh, wot two idiots you durned
    fools have been!"

I reckollect that they allowed we 'd made
    a big mistake,—
They otter knowed us tenderfoots wuz sure
    to make a break!
An', while Modjesky stated we wuz some-
    what off our base,
I half opined she liked it, by the look upon
    her face.
I reckollect that Hoover regretted he done
    wrong
In throwin' that there actor through a vista
    ten miles long.
I reckollect we all shuck hands, and ordered
    vin frappay,—
And I never shall forget the head I had on
    me next day!

I have n't seen Modjesky since; I 'm hopin'
    to again.
She 's goin' to show in Denver soon; I 'll go
    to see her then.
An' may be I shall speak to her, wich if I do
    't will be
About the old friend restin' by the mighty
    Western sea,—

A simple man, perhaps, but good ez gold and
    true ez steel;
He could whip his weight in wildcats, and
    you never heerd him squeal;
Good to the helpless and the weak; a brave
    an' manly heart
A cyclone could n't phase, but any child could
    rend apart;
So like the mountain pine, that dares the
    storm wich sweeps along,
But rocks the winds uv summer-time, an'
    sings a soothin' song.

TELLING THE BEES

O UT of the house where the slumberer lay
Grandfather came one summer day,
And under the pleasant orchard trees
He spake this wise to the murmuring bees:
   "The clover-bloom that kissed her feet
     And the posie-bed where she used to play
   Have honey store, but none so sweet
     As ere our little one went away.
O bees, sing soft, and, bees, sing low;
For she is gone who loved you so."

A wonder fell on the listening bees
Under those pleasant orchard trees,
And in their toil that summer day
Ever their murmuring seemed to say:

"Child, O child, the grass is cool,
    And the posies are waking to hear the
        song
Of the bird that swings by the shaded
    pool,
    Waiting for one that tarrieth long."
'T was so they called to the little one then,
As if to call her back again.

O gentle bees, I have come to say
That grandfather fell asleep to-day,
And we know by the smile on grandfather's
    face
He has found his dear one's biding-place.
    So, bees, sing soft, and, bees, sing low,
        As over the honey-fields you sweep,—
    To the trees abloom and the flowers ablow
        Sing of grandfather fast asleep;
And ever beneath these orchard trees
Find cheer and shelter, gentle bees.

THE TEA-GOWN

M Y lady has a tea-gown
   That is wondrous fair to see,—
It is flounced and ruffed and plaited and
   puffed,
  As a tea-gown ought to be;
And I thought she must be jesting
  Last night at supper when
She remarked, by chance, that it came from
   France,
  And had cost but two pounds ten.

Had she told me fifty shillings,
  I might (and would n't you?)
Have referred to that dress in a way folks
   express
  By an eloquent dash or two;
But the guileful little creature
  Knew well her tactics when
She casually said that that dream in red
  Had cost but two pounds ten.

Yet our home is all the brighter
   For that dainty, sentient thing,
That floats away where it properly may,
   And clings where it ought to cling;
And I count myself the luckiest
   Of all us married men
That I have a wife whose joy in life
   Is a gown at two pounds ten.

It is n't the gown compels me
   Condone this venial sin;
It 's the pretty face above the lace,
   And the gentle heart within.
And with her arms about me
   I say, and say again,
"'T was wondrous cheap,"— and I think a
    heap
   Of that gown at two pounds ten!

DOCTORS

'TIS quite the thing to say and sing
    Gross libels on the doctor,—
To picture him an ogre grim
    Or humbug-pill concocter;
Yet it 's in quite another light
    My friendly pen would show him,
Glad that it may with verse repay
    Some part of what I owe him.

When one 's all right, he 's prone to spite
    The doctor's peaceful mission;
But when he 's sick, it 's loud and quick
    He bawls for a physician.
With other things, the doctor brings
    Sweet babes, our hearts to soften:
Though I have four, I pine for more,—
    Good doctor, pray come often!

What though he sees death and disease
  Run riot all around him?
Patient and true, and valorous too,
  Such have I always found him.
Where'er he goes, he soothes our woes;
  And when skill's unavailing,
And death is near, his words of cheer
  Support our courage failing.

In ancient days they used to praise
  The godlike art of healing,—
An art that then engaged all men
  Possessed of sense and feeling.
Why, Raleigh, he was glad to be
  Famed for a quack elixir;
And Digby sold, as we are told,
  A charm for folk lovesick, sir.

Napoleon knew a thing or two,
  And clearly *he* was partial
To doctors, for in time of war
  He chose one for a marshal.
In our great cause a doctor was
  The first to pass death's portal,
And Warren's name at once became
  A beacon and immortal.

A heap, indeed, of what we read
　　By doctors is provided;
For to those groves Apollo loves
　　Their leaning is decided.
Deny who may that Rabelais
　　Is first in wit and learning,
And yet all smile and marvel while
　　His brilliant leaves they 're turning.

How Lever's pen has charmed all men!
　　How touching Rab's short story!
And I will stake my all that Drake
　　Is still the schoolboy's glory.
A doctor-man it was began
　　Great Britain's great museum,—
The treasures there are all so rare,
　　It drives me wild to see 'em!

There 's Cuvier, Parr, and Rush; they are
　　Big monuments to learning.
To Mitchell's prose (how smooth it flows!)
　　We all are fondly turning.
Tomes might be writ of that keen wit
　　Which Abernethy 's famed for;
With bread-crumb pills he cured the ills
　　Most doctors now get blamed for.

In modern times the noble rhymes
    Of Holmes, a great physician,
Have solace brought and wisdom taught
    To hearts of all condition.
The sailor, bound for Puget Sound,
    Finds pleasure still unfailing,
If he but troll the barcarole
    Old Osborne wrote on Whaling.

If there were need, I could proceed
    Ad naus. with this prescription,
But, *inter nos,* a larger dose
    Might give you fits conniption;
Yet, ere I end, there 's one dear friend
    I 'd hold before these others,
For he and I in years gone by
    Have chummed around like brothers.

Together we have sung in glee
    The songs old Horace made for
Our genial craft, together quaffed
    What bowls that doctor paid for!
I love the rest, but love him best;
    And, were not times so pressing,
I 'd buy and send — you smile, old friend?
    Well, then, here goes my blessing.

61

BARBARA

BLITHE was the youth that summer day,
  As he smote at the ribs of earth,
And he plied his pick with a merry click,
  And he whistled anon in mirth;
And the constant thought of his dear one's
    face
Seemed to illumine that ghostly place.

The gaunt earth envied the lover's joy,
  And she moved, and closed on his head:
With no one nigh and with never a cry
  The beautiful boy lay dead;
And the treasure he sought for his sweetheart
    fair
Crumbled, and clung to his glorious hair.

Fifty years is a mighty space
   In the human toil for bread;
But to Love and to Death 't is merely a
     breath,
   A dream that is quickly sped,—
Fifty years, and the fair lad lay
Just as he fell that summer day.

At last came others in quest of gold,
   And hewed in that mountain place;
And deep in the ground one time they found
   The boy with the smiling face:
All uncorrupt by the pitiless air,
He lay, with his crown of golden hair.

They bore him up to the sun again,
   And laid him beside the brook,
And the folk came down from the busy town
   To wonder and prate and look;
And so, to a world that knew him not,
The boy came back to the old-time spot.

Old Barbara hobbled among the rest,—
   Wrinkled and bowed was she,—
And she gave a cry, as she fared anigh,
   " At last he is come to me!"

And she kneeled by the side of the dead boy
     there,
And she kissed his lips, and she stroked his
     hair.

" Thine eyes are sealed, O dearest one !
     And better it is 't is so,
Else thou might'st see how harsh with me
     Dealt Life thou couldst not know:
Kindlier Death has kept *thee* fair;
The sorrow of Life hath been *my* share."

Barbara bowed her aged face,
     And fell on the breast of her dead;
And the golden hair of her dear one there
     Caressed her snow-white head.
Oh, Life is sweet, with its touch of pain;
But sweeter the Death that joined those
     twain.

THE CAFÉ MOLINEAU

THE Café Molineau is where
    A dainty little minx
Serves God and men as best she can
    By serving meats and drinks.
Oh, such an air the creature has,
    And such a pretty face!
I took delight that autumn night
    In hanging round the place.

I know but very little French
    (I have not long been here);
But when she spoke, her meaning broke
    Full sweetly on my ear.
Then, too, she seemed to understand
    Whatever I 'd to say,
Though most I knew was " oony poo,"
    "Bong zhoor," and "see voo play."

The female wit is always quick,
   And of all womankind
'T is here in France that you, perchance,
   The keenest wits shall find;
And here you 'll find that subtle gift,
   That rare, distinctive touch,
Combined with grace of form and face,
   That glads men overmuch.

"Our girls at home," I mused aloud,
   "Lack either that or this;
They don't combine the arts divine
   As does the Gallic miss.
Far be it from me to malign
   Our belles across the sea,
And yet I 'll swear none can compare
   With this ideal She."

And then I praised her dainty foot
   In very awful French,
And parleywood in guileful mood
   Until the saucy wench
Tossed back her haughty auburn head,
   And froze me with disdain:
"There are on me no flies," said she,
   "For I come from Bangor, Maine!"

66

HOLLY AND IVY

HOLLY standeth in ye house
    When that Noel draweth near;
Evermore at ye door
Standeth Ivy, shivering sore
    In ye night wind bleak and drear;
And, as weary hours go by,
Doth ye one to other cry.

"Sister Holly," Ivy quoth,
    "What is that within you see?
To and fro doth ye glow
Of ye yule-log flickering go;
    Would its warmth did cherish me!
Where thou bidest is it warm;
I am shaken of ye storm."

"Sister Ivy," Holly quoth,
  "Brightly burns the yule-log here,
And love brings beauteous things,
While a guardian angel sings
  To the babes that slumber near;
But, O Ivy! tell me now,
What without there seest thou?"

"Sister Holly," Ivy quoth,
  "With fair music comes ye Morn,
And afar burns ye Star
Where ye wondering shepherds are,
  And the Shepherd King is born:
'Peace on earth, good-will to men,'
Angels cry, and cry again."

Holly standeth in ye house
  When that Noel draweth near;
Clambering o'er yonder door,
Ivy standeth evermore;
  And to them that rightly hear
Each one speaketh of ye love
That outpoureth from Above.

THE BOLTONS, 22

WHEN winter nights are grewsome,
    and the heavy, yellow fog
Gives to Piccadilly semblance of a dank,
    malarious bog;
When a demon, with companion in simili-
    tude of bell,
Goes round informing people he has crum-
    pets for to sell;
When a weird, asthmatic minstrel haunts
    your door for hours along,
Until you 've paid him tu'pence for the thing
    he calls a song,—
When, in short, the world 's against you,
    and you 'd give that world, and more,
To lay your weary heart at rest upon your
    native shore,
There 's happily one saving thing for you
    and yours to do:
Go call on Isaac Henderson, The Boltons, 22.

The place is all so cheery and so warm, I
    love to spend
My evenings in communion with the genial
    host, my friend.
One sees *chefs d'œuvre* of masters in pro-
    fusion on the walls,
And a monster canine swaggers up and
    down the spacious halls;
There are divers things of beauty to astound,
    instruct, and please,
And everywhere assurance of contentment
    and of ease:
But best of all the gentle hearts I meet with
    in the place,—
The host's good-fellowship, his wife's sin-
    cere and modest grace;
Why, if there be cordiality that warms you
    through and through,
It 's found at Isaac Henderson's, The Bol-
    tons, 22.

My favorite room 's the study that is on the
    second floor;
And there we sit in judgment on men and
    things galore.

70

The fire burns briskly in the grate, and sheds
    a genial glare
On me, who most discreetly have preëmpted
    Isaac's chair,—
A big, low chair, with grateful springs, and
    curious device
To keep a fellow's cerebellum comf'table and
    nice.
A shade obscures the functions of the stately
    lamp, in spite
Of Mrs. Henderson's demands for somewhat
    more of light;
But he and I demur, and say a mystic gloom
    will do
For winter-night communion at the Bol-
    tons, 22.

Sometimes he reads me Browning, or from
    Bryant culls a bit,
And sometimes plucks a gem from Hood's
    philosophy and wit ;
And oftentimes I tell him yarns, and (what I
    fear is worse)
Recite him sundry specimens of woolly
    Western verse.

71

And while his muse and mine transcend the
  bright Horatian's stars,
He smokes his modest pipe, and I — I smoke
  his choice cigars !
For best of mild Havanas this considerate host
  supplies, —
The proper brand, the proper shade, and
  quite the proper size;
And so I buckle down and smoke and
  smoke, — and so will you,
If ever you 're invited to the Boltons, 22.

But, oh! the best of worldly joys is as a
  dream short-lived :
'T is twelve o'clock, and Robinson reports
  our cab arrived.
A last libation ere we part, and hands all
  round, and then
A cordial invitation to us both to come again.
So home through Piccadilly and through
  Oxford Street we jog,
On slippery, noisy pavements and in blind-
  ing, choking fog, —
The same old route through Circus, Square,
  and Quadrant we retrace,

Till we reach the princely mansion known
    as 20 Alfred Place ;
And then we seek our feathery beds of cotton
    to renew
In dreams the sweet distractions of the Bol-
    tons, 22.

God bless you, good friend Isaac, and your
    lovely, gracious wife;
May health and wealth attend you, and hap-
    piness, through life;
And as you sit of evenings that quiet room
    within,
Know that in spirit I shall be your guest as
    I have been.
So fill and place beside that chair that dainty
    claret-cup;
Methinks that ghostly hands shall take the
    tempting offering up,
That ghostly lips shall touch the bowl and
    quaff the ruby wine,
Pledging in true affection this toast to thee
    and thine:
" May God's best blessings fall as falls the
    gentle, gracious dew
Upon the kindly household at the Boltons, 22 !"

DIBDIN'S GHOST

D EAR wife, last midnight, whilst I read
  The tomes you so despise,
A spectre rose beside the bed,
  And spake in this true wise:
"From Canaan's beatific coast
  I 've come to visit thee,
For I am Frognall Dibdin's ghost,"
  Says Dibdin's ghost to me.

I bade him welcome, and we twain
  Discussed with buoyant hearts
The various things that appertain
  To bibliomaniac arts.
"Since you are fresh from t' other side,
  Pray tell me of that host
That treasured books before they died,"
  Says I to Dibdin's ghost.

74

"They 've entered into perfect rest;
  For in the life they 've won
There are no auctions to molest,
  No creditors to dun.
Their heavenly rapture has no bounds
  Beside that jasper sea;
It is a joy unknown to Lowndes,"
  Says Dibdin's ghost to me.

Much I rejoiced to hear him speak
  Of biblio-bliss above,
For I am one of those who seek
  What bibliomaniacs love.
"But tell me, for I long to hear
  What doth concern me most,
Are wives admitted to that sphere?"
  Says I to Dibdin's ghost.

"The women folk are few up there;
  For 't were not fair, you know,
That they our heavenly joy should share
  Who vex us here below.
The few are those who have been kind
  To husbands such as we;
They knew our fads, and did n't mind,"
  Says Dibdin's ghost to me.

"But what of those who scold at us
  When we would read in bed?
Or, wanting victuals, make a fuss
  If we buy books instead?
And what of those who 've dusted not
  Our motley pride and boast,—
Shall they profane that sacred spot?"
  Says I to Dibdin's ghost.

"Oh, no! they tread that other path,
  Which leads where torments roll,
And worms, yes, bookworms, vent their
    wrath
  Upon the guilty soul.
Untouched of bibliomaniac grace,
  That saveth such as we,
They wallow in that dreadful place,"
  Says Dibdin's ghost to me.

"To my dear wife will I recite
  What things I 've heard you say;
She 'll let me read the books by night
  She 's let me buy by day.
For we together by and by
  Would join that heavenly host;
She 's earned a rest as well as I,"
  Says I to Dibdin's ghost.

THE BOTTLE AND THE BIRD

ONCE on a time a friend of mine pre-
vailed on me to go
To see the dazzling splendors of a sinful
ballet show;
And after we had revelled in the saltatory
sights,
We sought a neighboring *café* for more tan-
gible delights.
When I demanded of my friend what viands
he preferred,
He quoth: "A large cold bottle, and a small
hot bird!"

Fool that I was, I did not know what anguish hidden lies
Within the morceau that allures the nostrils
and the eyes!
There is a glorious candor in an honest quart
of wine,

77

A certain inspiration which I cannot well
    define!
How it bubbles, how it sparkles, how its
    gurgling seems to say:
"Come! on a tide of rapture let me float
    your soul away!"

But the crispy, steaming mouthful that is
    spread upon your plate,—
How it discounts human sapience and satir-
    izes fate!
You would n't think a thing so small could
    cause the pains and aches
That certainly accrue to him that of that
    thing partakes;
To me, at least, (a guileless wight!) it never
    once occurred
What horror was encompassed in that small
    hot bird.

Oh; what a head I had on me when I awoke
    next day,
And what a firm conviction of intestinal
    decay!

What seas of mineral water and of bromide
    I applied
To quench those fierce volcanic fires that
    rioted inside!
And, oh, the thousand solemn, awful vows
    I plighted then
Never to tax my system with a small hot
    bird again!

The doctor seemed to doubt that birds could
    worry people so,
But, bless him! since I ate the bird, I guess
    I ought to know!
The acidous condition of my stomach, so
    he said,
Bespoke a vinous irritant that amplified my
    head,
And, ergo, the causation of the thing, as he
    inferred,
Was the large cold bottle,— *not* the small
    hot bird.

Of course I know it was n't, and I 'm sure
    you 'll say I 'm right
If ever it has been your wont to train around
    at night.

79

How sweet is retrospection when one's
 heart is bathed in wine,
And before its balmy breath how do the ills
 of life decline!
How the gracious juices drown what griefs
 would vex a mortal breast,
And float the flattered soul into the port of
 dreamless rest!

But you, O noxious, pigmy bird! whether
 it be you fly,
Or paddle in the stagnant pools that swelter-
 ing, festering lie,—
I curse you and your evil kind for that you
 do me wrong,
Engendering poisons that corrupt my petted
 muse of song;
Go, get thee hence! and never more discom-
 fit me and mine,—
I fain would barter all thy brood for one
 sweet draught of wine!

So hither come, O sportive youth! when
 fades the telltale day,—
Come hither, with your fillets and your
 wreaths of posies gay;

We shall unloose the fragrant seas of seeth-
    ing, frothing wine
Which now the cobwebbed glass and en-
    vious wire and corks confine,
And midst the pleasing revelry the praises
    shall be heard
Of the large cold bottle,— *not* the small hot
    bird!

AN ECLOGUE FROM VIRGIL

[The exile Melibœus finds Tityrus in possession of his own farm, restored to him by the Emperor Augustus, and a conversation ensues. The poem is in praise of Augustus, peace, and pastoral life.]

MELIBŒUS

TITYRUS, all in the shade of the wide-
    spreading beech-tree reclining,
  Sweet is that music you 've made on your
    pipe that is oaten and slender;
Exiles from home, you beguile our hearts
    from their hopeless repining,
  As you sing Amaryllis the while in pas-
    torals tuneful and tender.

TITYRUS

A god — yes, a god, I declare — vouchsafes
    me these pleasant conditions,
  And often I gayly repair with a tender
    white lamb to his altar;

He gives me the leisure to play my greatly
    admired compositions,
  While my heifers go browsing all day,
    unhampered of bell and of halter.

MELIBŒUS

I do not begrudge you repose; I simply ad-
    mit I 'm confounded
  To find you unscathed of the woes of pil-
    lage and tumult and battle.
To exile and hardship devote, and by mer-
    ciless enemies hounded,
  I drag at this wretched old goat and coax
    on my famishing cattle.
Oh, often the omens presaged the horrors
    which now overwhelm me —
But, come, if not elsewise engaged, who *is*
    this good deity, tell me!

TITYRUS (reminiscently)

The city — the city called Rome, with my
    head full of herding and tillage,
  I used to compare with my home, these
    pastures wherein you now wander;

But I did n't take long to find out that the
    city surpasses the village
  As the cypress surpasses the sprout that
    thrives in the thicket out yonder.

MELIBŒUS

Tell me, good gossip, I pray, what led you
    to visit the city?

TITYRUS

  Liberty! which on a day regarded my lot
    with compassion;
My age and distresses, forsooth, compelled
    that proud mistress to pity,
  That had snubbed the attentions of youth
    in most reprehensible fashion.
Oh, happy, thrice happy, the day when the
    cold Galatea forsook me;
And equally happy, I say, the hour when
    that other girl took me!

MELIBŒUS (slyly, as if addressing the damsel)

So now, Amaryllis, the truth of your ill-
    disguised grief I discover!
  You pined for a favorite youth with city-
    fied damsels hobnobbing;

And soon your surroundings partook of your
    grief for your recusant lover,—
    The pine-trees, the copse, and the brook,
      for Tityrus ever went sobbing.

TITYRUS

Melibœus, what else could I do ? Fate doled
    me no morsel of pity;
    My toil was all vain the year through, no
      matter how earnest or clever,
Till, at last, came that god among men, that
    king from that wonderful city,
    And quoth : "Take your homesteads again ;
      they are yours and your assigns' forever!"

MELIBŒUS

Happy, oh, happy old man! rich in what 's
    better than money,—
    Rich in contentment, you can gather sweet
      peace by mere listening;
Bees with soft murmurings go hither and
    thither for honey,
    Cattle all gratefully low in pastures where
      fountains are glistening —
Hark! in the shade of that rock the pruner
    with singing rejoices,—

85

The dove in the elm and the flock of wood-
　　pigeons hoarsely repining,
The plash of the sacred cascade,—ah, rest-
　　ful, indeed, are these voices,
　　Tityrus, all in the shade of your wide-
　　spreading beech-tree reclining!

TITYRUS

And he who insures this to me—oh, craven
　　I were not to love him!
　　Nay, rather the fish of the sea shall vacate
　　the water they swim in,
The stag quit his bountiful grove to graze
　　in the ether above him,
　　While folk antipodean rove along with
　　their children and women!

MELIBŒUS (suddenly recalling his own misery)

But we who are exiled must go; and whither
　　—ah, whither—God knoweth!
　　Some into those regions of snow or of
　　desert where Death reigneth only;
Some off to the country of Crete, where rapid
　　Oaxes down floweth;
　　And desperate others retreat to Britain, the
　　bleak isle and lonely.

Dear land of my birth! shall I see the horde
   of invaders oppress thee?
  Shall the wealth that outspringeth from thee
   by the hand of the alien be squandered?
Dear cottage wherein I was born! shall another in conquest possess thee,
  Another demolish in scorn the fields and
   the groves where I 've wandered?
My flock! nevermore shall you graze on that
   furze-covered hillside above me;
  Gone, gone are the halcyon days when
   my reed piped defiance to sorrow!
Nevermore in the vine-covered grot shall I
   sing of the loved ones that love me,—
  Let yesterday's peace be forgot in dread of
   the stormy to-morrow!

TITYRUS

But rest you this night with me here; my
   bed,—we will share it together,
  As soon as you 've tasted my cheer, my
   apples and chestnuts and cheeses;
The evening already is nigh,—the shadows
   creep over the heather,
  And the smoke is rocked up to the sky to
   the lullaby song of the breezes.

ASHES ON THE SLIDE

WHEN Jim and Bill and I were boys a
many years ago,
How gayly did we use to hail the coming
of the snow!
Our sleds, fresh painted red and with their
runners round and bright,
Seemed to respond right briskly to our
clamor of delight
As we dragged them up the slippery road
that climbed the rugged hill
Where perched the old frame meetin'-house,
so solemn-like and still.

Ah, coasting in those days — those good old
days — was fun indeed!
Sleds at that time I 'd have you know were
paragons of speed!

And if the hill got bare in spots, as hills will
    do, why then
We 'd haul on ice and snow to patch those
    bald spots up again;
But, oh! with what sad certainty our spirits
    would subside
When Deacon Frisbee sprinkled ashes where
    we used to slide!

The deacon he would roll his eyes and gnash
    his toothless gums,
And clear his skinny throat, and twirl his
    saintly, bony thumbs,
And tell you: "When I wuz a boy, they
    taught me to eschew
The godless, ribald vanities which modern
    youth pursue!
The pathway that leads down to hell is slip-
    pery, straight, and wide;
And Satan lurks for prey where little boys
    are wont to slide!"

Now, he who ever in his life has been a little
    boy
Will not reprove me when he hears the lan-
    guage I employ

89

To stigmatize as wickedness the deacon's
    zealous spite
In interfering with the play wherein we
    found delight;
And so I say, with confidence, not unalloyed
    of pride:
"Gol durn the man who sprinkles ashes
    where the youngsters slide!"

But Deacon Frisbee long ago went to his
    lasting rest,
His money well invested in farm mortgages
    out West;
Bill, Jim, and I, no longer boys, have learned
    through years of strife
That the troubles of the little boy pursue the
    man through life;
That here and there along the course wherein
    we hoped to glide
Some envious hand has sprinkled ashes just
    to spoil our slide!

And that malicious, envious hand is not the
    deacon's now.
Grim, ruthless Fate, that evil sprite none
    other is than thou!

Riches and honors, peace and care come at
    thy beck and go;
The soul, elate with joy to-day, to-morrow
    writhes in woe;
And till a man has turned his face unto the
    wall and died,
He must expect to get his share of ashes on
    his slide!

THE LOST CUPID OF MOSCHUS

" CUPID!" Venus went a-crying;
    "Cupid, whither dost thou stray?
Tell me, people, hither hieing,
    Have you seen my runaway?
    Speak,— my kiss shall be your pay!
Yes, and sweets more gratifying,
    If you bring him back to-day.

"Cupid," Venus went a-calling,
    "Is a rosy little youth,
But his beauty is inthralling.
    He will speak you fair, in sooth,
    Wheedle you with glib untruth,—
Honey-like his words; but galling
    Are his deeds, and full of ruth!

" Cupid's hair is curling yellow,
　　And he hath a saucy face;
With his chubby hands the fellow
　　Shooteth into farthest space,
　　Heedless of all time and place;
King and squire and punchinello
　　He delighteth to abase!

"Nude and winged the prankish blade is,
　　And he speedeth everywhere,
Vexing gentlemen and ladies,
　　Callow youths and damsels fair
　　Whom he catcheth unaware;—
Venturing even into Hades,
　　He hath sown his torments there!

"For that bow, that bow and quiver,—
　　Oh, they are a cruel twain!
Thinking of them makes me shiver.
　　Oft, with all his might and main,
　　Cupid sends those darts profane
Whizzing through my heart and liver,
　　Setting fire to every vein!

"And the torch he carries blazing,—
 Truly 't is a tiny one;
Yet, that tiny torch upraising,
 Cupid scarifies the sun!
 Ah, good people, there is none
Knows what mischief most amazing
 Cupid's evil torch hath done!

"Show no mercy when you find him!
 Spite of every specious plea
And of all his whimpering, bind him!
 Full of flatteries is he;
 Armed with treachery, *cap-a-pie,*
He 'll play 'possum; never mind him,—
 March him straightway back to me!

"Bow and arrows and sweet kisses
 He will offer you, no doubt;
But beware those proffered blisses,—
 They are venomous throughout!
 Seize and bind him fast about;
Mind you,— most important this is:
 Bind him, bring him, but— watch out!"

CHRISTMAS EVE

OH, hush thee, little Dear-my-Soul,
    The evening shades are falling,—
Hush thee, my dear, dost thou not hear
    The voice of the Master calling?

Deep lies the snow upon the earth,
    But all the sky is ringing
With joyous song, and all night long
    The stars shall dance, with singing.

Oh, hush thee, little Dear-my-Soul,
    And close thine eyes in dreaming,
And angels fair shall lead thee where
    The singing stars are beaming.

A shepherd calls his little lambs,
    And he longeth to caress them;
He bids them rest upon his breast,
    That his tender love may bless them.

So, hush thee, little Dear-my-Soul,
    Whilst evening shades are falling,
And above the song of the heavenly throng
    Thou shalt hear the Master calling.

CARLSBAD

DEAR Palmer, just a year ago we did
   the Carlsbad cure,
Which, though it be exceeding slow, is as
   exceeding sure;
To corpulency you were prone, dyspepsia
   bothered me,—
You tipped the beam at twenty stone and I
   at ten stone three!
The cure, they told us, works both ways:
   it makes the fat man lean;
The thin man, after many days, achieves a
   portly mien;
And though it 's true you still are fat, while
   I am like a crow,—
All skin and feathers,— what of that? The
   cure takes time, you know.

The Carlsbad scenery is sublime,— that 's
    what the guide-books say;
We did not think so at that time, nor think
    I so to-day!
The bluffs that squeeze the panting town
    permit no pleasing views,
But weigh the mortal spirits down and give
    a chap the blues.
With nothing to amuse us then or mitigate
    our spleen,
We rose and went to bed again, with three
    bad meals between;
And constantly we made our moan,— ah,
    none so drear as we,
When you were weighing twenty stone
    and I but ten stone three!

We never scaled the mountain-side, for walk-
    ing was my bane,
And you were much too big to ride the
    mules that there obtain;
And so we loitered in the shade, with Israel
    out in force,
Or through the Pupp'sche allee strayed and
    heard the band discourse.

98

Sometimes it pleased us to recline upon the
    Tepl's brink,
Or watch the bilious human line file round
    to get a drink;
Anon the portier's piping tone embittered
    you and me,
When you were weighing twenty stone and
    I but ten stone three!

And oh! those awful things to eat! No pud-
    ding, cake, or pie,
But just a little dab of meat, and crusts ab-
    surdly dry;
Then, too, that water twice a day,— one
    swallow was enough
To take one's appetite away,—the tepid,
    awful stuff!
Tortured by hunger's cruel stings, I'd little
    else to do
Than feast my eyes upon the things pre-
    scribed and cooked for you.
The goodies went to you alone, the husks
    all fell to me,
When you were weighing twenty stone and
    I weighed ten stone three.

99

Yet happy days! and rapturous ills! and
    sweetly dismal date!
When, sandwiched in between those hills,
    we twain bemoaned our fate.
The little woes we suffered then like mists
    have sped away,
And I were glad to share again those ills
    with you to-day,—
To flounder in those rains of June that flood
    that Austrian vale,
To quaff that tepid Kaiserbrunn and starve
    on victuals stale!
And often, leagues and leagues away from
    where we suffered then,
With envious yearnings I survey what can-
    not be again!

And often in my quiet home, through dim
    and misty eyes,
I seem to see that curhaus dome blink at the
    radiant skies;
I seem to hear that Wiener band above the
    Tepl's roar,—
To feel the pressure of your hand and hear
    your voice once more;

And, better yet, my heart is warm with
    thoughts of you and yours,
For friendship hath a sweeter charm than
    thrice ten thousand cures!
So I am happy to have known that time
    across the sea
When you were weighing twenty stone and
    I weighed ten stone three.

RED

ANY color, so long as it 's red,
  Is the color that suits me best,
Though I will allow there is much to be said
  For yellow and green and the rest;
But the feeble tints which some affect
  In the things they make or buy
Have never — I say it with all respect —
  Appealed to my critical eye.

There 's that in red that warmeth the blood,
  And quickeneth a man within,
And bringeth to speedy and perfect bud
  The germs of original sin;
So, though I 'm properly born and bred,
  I 'll own, with a certain zest,
That any color, so long as it 's red,
  Is the color that suits me best.

For where is the color that can compare
    With the blush of a buxom lass;
Or where such warmth as of the hair
    Of the genuine white horse class?
And, lo! reflected within this cup
    Of cheery Bordeaux I see
What inspiration girdeth me up,—
    Yes, red is the color for me!

Through acres and acres of art I 've strayed
    In Italy, Germany, France;
On many a picture a master has made
    I 've squandered a passing glance:
Marines I hate, madonnas and
    Those Dutch freaks I detest;
But the peerless daubs of my native land,—
    They 're red, and I like them best.

'T is little I care how folk deride,—
    I 'm backed by the West, at least;
And we are free to say that we can't abide
    The tastes that obtain down East;
And we 're mighty proud to have it said
    That here in the versatile West
Most any color, so long as it 's red,
    Is the color that suits us best.

103

AT CHEYENNE

YOUNG Lochinvar came in from the west,
   With fringe on his trousers and fur on
   his vest;
The width of his hat-brim could nowhere be
      beat,
His No. 10 brogans were chuck full of feet,
His girdle was horrent with pistols and
      things,
And he flourished a handful of aces on kings.

The fair Mariana sate watching a star,
When who should turn up but the young
      Lochinvar!
Her pulchritude gave him a pectoral glow,
And he reined up his hoss with stentorian
      "Whoa!"
Then turned on the maiden a rapturous grin,
And modestly asked if he might n't step in.

104

With presence of mind that was marvellous
    quite,
The fair Mariana replied that he might;
So in through the portal rode young Lochin-
    var,
Preëmpted the claim, and cleaned out the
    bar.
Though the justice allowed he wa'n't wholly
    to blame,
He taxed him ten dollars and costs, just the
    same.

THE PNEUMOGASTRIC NERVE

UPON an average, twice a week,
    When anguish clouds my brow,
My good physician friend I seek
    To know " what ails me now."
He taps me on the back and chest,
    And scans my tongue for bile,
And lays an ear against my breast
    And listens there awhile;
Then is he ready to admit
    That all he can observe
Is something wrong inside, to wit:
    My pneumogastric nerve!

Now, when these Latin names within
    Dyspeptic hulks like mine
Go wrong, a fellow should begin
    To draw what's called the line.

It seems, however, that this same,
  Which in my hulks abounds,
Is not, despite its awful name,
  So fatal as it sounds;
Yet of all torments known to me,
  I 'll say without reserve,
There is no torment like to thee,
  Thou pneumogastric nerve!

This subtle, envious nerve appears
  To be a patient foe,—
It waited nearly forty years
  Its chance to lay me low;
Then, like some blithering blast of hell,
  It struck this guileless bard,
And in that evil hour I fell
  Prodigious far and hard.
Alas! what things I dearly love—
  Pies, puddings, and preserves—
Are sure to rouse the vengeance of
  All pneumogastric nerves!

Oh that I could remodel man!
  I 'd end these cruel pains
By hitting on a different plan
  From that which now obtains.

The stomach, greatly amplified,
　　Anon should occupy
The all of that domain inside
　　Where heart and lungs now lie.
But, first of all, I should depose
　　That diabolic curve
And author of my thousand woes,
　　The pneumogastric nerve!

TELKA

THROUGH those golden summer days
   Our twin flocks were wont to graze
On the hillside, which the sun
Rested lovingly upon,—
Telka's flock and mine; and we
Sung our songs in rapturous glee,
Idling in the pleasant shade
Which the solemn Yew-tree made,
While the Brook anear us played,
And a white Rose, ghost-like, grew
In the shadow of the Yew.

Telka loved me passing well;
How I loved her none can tell!
How I love her none may know,—
Oh, that man loves woman so!

When she was not at my side,
Loud my heart in anguish cried,
And my lips, till she replied.
Yet they think to silence me,—
As if love could silenced be!
Fool were I, and fools were they!
Still I wend my lonely way,
"Telka," evermore I cry;
Answer me the woods and sky,
And the weary years go by.

Telka, she was passing fair;
And the glory of her hair
Was such glory as the sun
With his blessing casts upon
Yonder lonely mountain height,
Lifting up to bid good-night
To her sovereign in the west,
Sinking wearily to rest,
Drowsing in that golden sea
Where the realms of Dreamland be.

So our love to fulness grew,
Whilst beneath the solemn Yew
Ghost-like paled the Rose of white,
As it were some fancied sight
Blanched it with a dread affright.

Telka, she was passing fair;
And our peace was perfect there
Till, enchanted by her smile,
Lurked the South Wind there awhile,
Underneath that hillside tree
Where with singing idled we,
And I heard the South Wind say
Flattering words to her that day
Of a city far away.
But the Yew-tree crouched as though
It were like to whisper No
To the words the South Wind said
As he smoothed my Telka's head.
And the Brook, all pleading, cried
To the dear one at my side:
"Linger always where I am;
Stray not thence, O cosset lamb!
Wander not where shadows deep
On the treacherous quicksands sleep,
And the haunted waters leap;
Be thou ware the waves that flow
Toward the prison pool below,
Where, beguiled from yonder sky,
Captive moonbeams shivering lie,
And at dawn of morrow die."
So the Brook to Telka cried,

111

But my Telka naught replied;
And, as in a strange affright,
Paled the Rose a ghostlier white.

When anon the North Wind came,—
Rudely blustering Telka's name,
And he kissed the leaves that grew
Round about the trembling Yew,—
Kissed and romped till, blushing red,
All one day in terror fled,
And the white Rose hung her head;
Coming to our trysting spot,
Long I called; she answered not.
"Telka!" pleadingly I cried
Up and down the mountain-side
Where we twain were wont to bide.

There were those who thought that I
Could be silenced with a lie,
And they told me Telka's name
Should be spoken now with shame;
"She is lost to us and thee,"—
That is what they said to me.

"Is my Telka lost?" quoth I.
"On this hilltop shall I cry,

So that she may hear and then
Find her way to me again.
The South Wind spoke a lie that day;
All deceived, she lost her way;
Yonder where the shadows sleep
'Mongst the haunted waves that leap
Over treacherous quicksands deep,
And where captive moonbeams lie
Doomed at morrow's dawn to die,
She is lost, and that is all;
I will search for her, and call."

Summer comes and winter goes,
Buds the Yew and blooms the Rose;
All the others are anear,—
Only Telka is not here!
Gone the peace and love I knew
Sometime 'neath the hillside Yew;
And the Rose, that mocks me so,
I had crushed it long ago
But that Telka loved it then,
And shall soothe its terror when
She comes back to me again.
Call I, seek I everywhere
For my Telka, passing fair.

It is, oh, so many a year
I have called!   She does not hear,
Yet nor feared nor worn am I;
For I know that if I cry
She shall sometime hear my call.
She is lost, and that is all,—
She is lost in some far spot;
I have searched, and found it not.
Could she hear me calling, then
Would she come to me again;
For she loved me passing well,—
How I love her none can tell!
That is why these years I 've cried
"Telka!" on this mountain-side.
"Telka!" still I, pleading, cry;
Answer me the woods and sky,
And the lonely years go by.

On an evening dark and chill
Came a shadow up the hill,—
Came a spectre, grim and white
As a ghost that walks the night,
Grim and bowed, and with the cry
Of a wretch about to die,—
Came and fell and cried to me:
"It is Telka come!" said she.

So she fell and so she cried
On that lonely mountain-side
Where was Telka wont to bide.

"Who hath bribed those lips to lie?
Telka's face was fair," quoth I;
"Thine is furrowed with despair.
There is winter in thy hair;
But upon her beauteous head
Was there summer glory shed,—
Such a glory as the sun,
When his daily course is run,
Smiles upon this mountain height
As he kisses it good-night.
There was music in her tone,
Misery in thy voice alone.
They have bid thee lie to me.
Let me pass! Thou art not she!
Let my sorrow sacred be
Underneath this trysting tree!"

So in wrath I went my way,
And they came another day,—
Came another day, and said:
"Hush thy cry, for she is dead.

Yonder on the mountain-side
She is buried where she died,
Where you twain were wont to bide,
Where she came and fell and cried
Pardon that thy wrath denied;
And above her bosom grows
As in mockery the Rose:
It was white; but now 't is red,
And in shame it bows its head
Over sinful Telka dead."

So they thought to silence me,—
As if love could silenced be!
Fool were I, and fools were they!
Scornfully I went my way,
And upon the mountain- side
"Telka!" evermore I cried.
"Telka!" evermore I cry;
Answer me the woods and sky:
So the lonely years go by.

She is lost, and that is all;
Sometime she shall hear my call,
Hear my pleading call, and then
Find her way to me again.

PLAINT OF THE MISSOURI 'COON IN THE BERLIN ZOÖLOGICAL GARDENS

FRIEND, by the way you hump yourself
   you 're from the States, I know,
And born in old Mizzoorah, where the 'coons
   in plenty grow.
I, too, am native of that clime; but harsh,
   relentless fate
Has doomed me to an exile far from that
   noble State;
And I, who used to climb around, and swing
   from tree to tree,
Now lead a life of ignominious ease, as you
   can see.
Have pity, O compatriot mine! and bide a
   season near,
While I unfurl a dismal tale to catch your
   friendly ear.

My pedigree is noble: they used my grand-
sire's skin
To piece a coat for Patterson to warm him-
self within,—
Tom Patterson, of Denver; no ermine can
compare
With the grizzled robe that Democratic
statesman loves to wear.
Of such a grandsire I am come; and in the
County Cole
All up an ancient cottonwood our family had
its hole.
We envied not the liveried pomp nor proud
estate of kings,
As we hustled round from day to day in
search of bugs and things.

And when the darkness fell around, a mock-
ing-bird was nigh,
Inviting pleasant, soothing dreams with his
sweet lullaby;
And sometimes came the yellow dog to brag
around all night
That nary 'coon could wallop him in a stand-
up barrel fight.

We simply smiled and let him howl, for all
    Mizzoorians know
That ary 'coon can best a dog, if the coon
    gets half a show;
But we 'd nestle close and shiver when the
    mellow moon had ris'n,
And the hungry nigger sought our lair in
    hopes to make us his'n.

Raised as I was, it 's hardly strange I pine
    for those old days;
I cannot get acclimated, or used to German
    ways.
The victuals that they give me here may all
    be very fine
For vulgar, common palates, but they will
    not do for mine.
The 'coon that 's been accustomed to stanch
    Democratic cheer
Will not put up with onion tarts and sausage
    steeped in beer!
No; let the rest, for meat and drink, accede
    to slavish terms,
But send *me* back from whence I came, and
    let me grub for worms!

They come, these gaping Teutons do, on
    Sunday afternoons,
And wonder what I am,—alas, there are
    no German 'coons!
For if there were, I still might swing at home
    from tree to tree,
The symbol of Democracy, that 's woolly,
    blithe, and free.
And yet for what my captors are I would not
    change my lot,
For *I* have tasted liberty, these others, *they*
    have not;
So, even caged, the Democratic 'coon more
    glory feels
Than the conscript German puppets with
    their swords about their heels.

Well, give my love to Crittenden, to Clardy,
    and O'Neill,
To Jasper Burke and Colonel Jones, and
    tell 'em how I feel;
My compliments to Cockrill, Stephens, Switz-
    ler, Francis, Vest,
Bill Nelson, J. West Goodwin, Jedge Broad-
    head, and the rest.

Bid them be steadfast in the faith, and pay
    no heed at all
To Joe McCullagh's badinage or Chauncey
    Filley's gall;
And urge them to retaliate for what I 'm suf-
    fering here
By cinching all the alien class that wants its
    Sunday beer.

THE PARTRIDGE

AS beats the sun from mountain crest,
　　With "Pretty, pretty,"
Cometh the partridge from her nest.
The flowers threw kisses sweet to her
(For all the flowers that bloomed knew her);
Yet hasteneth she to mine and me,—
　　　　Ah, pretty, pretty!
　　　　Ah, dear little partridge!

And when I hear the partridge cry
　　So pretty, pretty,
Upon the house-top breakfast I.
She comes a-chirping far and wide.
And swinging from the mountain-side
I see and hear the dainty dear,—
　　　　Ah, pretty, pretty!
　　　　Ah, dear little partridge!

Thy nest 's inlaid with posies rare,
    And pretty, pretty,
Bloom violet, rose, and lily there;
The place is full of balmy dew
(The tears of flowers in love with you!);
And one and all, impassioned, call,
      "O pretty, pretty!
      O dear little partridge!"

Thy feathers they are soft and sleek,—
    So pretty, pretty!
Long is thy neck, and small thy beak,
The color of thy plumage far
More bright than rainbow colors are.
Sweeter than dove is she I love,—
      My pretty, pretty!
      My dear little partridge!

When comes the partridge from the tree,
    So pretty, pretty,
And sings her little hymn to me,
Why, all the world is cheered thereby,
The heart leaps up into the eye,
And Echo then gives back again
      Our "Pretty, pretty!"
      Our "Dear little partridge!"

Admitting thee most blest of all,
    And pretty, pretty,
The birds come with thee at thy call;
In flocks they come, and round thee play,
And this is what they seem to say: —
They say, and sing, each feathered thing,
    "Ah, pretty, pretty!
    Ah, dear little partridge!"

CORINTHIAN HALL

CORINTHIAN HALL is a tumble-down
   place,
Which some finical folks have pronounced
   a disgrace;
But once was a time when Corinthian Hall
Excited the rapture and plaudits of all,
      With its carpeted stairs,
      And its new yellow chairs,
And its stunning *ensemble* of citified airs.
Why, the Atchison Champion said 't was
   the best
Of Thespian temples extant in the West.

It was new, and was ours,— that was ages
   ago,
Before opry had spoiled the legitimate
   show,—

It was new, and was ours!   We could toss
    back the jeers
Our rivals had launched at our city for years.
      Corinthian Hall,
       Why, it discounted all
Other halls in the Valley, and well I recall
The night of the opening; from near and afar
Came the crowd to see Toodles performed
    by De Bar.

Oh, those days they were palmy, and never
    again
Shall earth see such genius as gladdened us
    then;
For actors were actors, and each one knew
    how
To whoop up his art in the sweat of his
    brow.
He 'd a tragedy air, and wore copious hair;
And when he ate victuals, he ordered 'em
    rare.
Dame Fortune ne'er feazed him,— in fact,
    never could
When liquor was handy and walking was
    good.

And the shows in those days!   Ah, how well
 I recall
The shows that I saw in Corinthian Hall!
Maggie Mitchell and Lotty were then in their
 prime;
And as for Jane Coombs, she was simply
 sublime;
And I 'm ready to swear there is none could
 compare
With Breslau in Borgia, supported by Fair;
While in passionate rôles it was patent to us
That the great John A. Stevens was *ne ultra
plus*.

And was there demand for the tribute of
 tears,
We had sweet Charlotte Thompson those
 halcyon years,
And wee Katie Putnam.   The savants allow
That the like of Kate Fisher ain't visible
 now.
What artist to-day have we equal to Rae,
Or to sturdy Jack Langrishe ?   God rest 'em,
 I say!
And when died Buchanan, the "St. Jo
 Gazette"

Opined that the sun of our drama had set.
Corinthian Hall was devoted to song
When the Barnabee concert troupe happened
　　along,
Or Ossian E. Dodge, or the Comical Brown,
Or the Holmans with William H. Crane
　　struck our town;
　　　　But the one special card
　　　　That hit us all hard
Was Caroline Richings and Peter Bernard;
And the bells of the Bergers still ring in my
　　ears;
And, oh, how I laughed at Sol Russell those
　　years!

The Haverly Minstrels were boss in those
　　days,
And our critics accorded them columns of
　　praise;
They 'd handsome mustaches and big cluster
　　rings,
And their shirt fronts were blazing with dia-
　　monds and things;
They gave a parade, and sweet music they
　　made

Every evening in front of the house where
    they played.
'Twixt posters and hand-bills the town was
    agog
For Primrose and West in their great statue
    clog.

Many years intervene, yet I 'm free to main-
    tain
That I doted on Chanfrau, McWade, and
    Frank Frayne;
Tom Stivers, the local, declared for a truth
That Mayo as Hamlet was better than Booth:
While in rôles that were thrillin', involving
    much killin',
Jim Wallick loomed up our ideal of a villain;
Mrs. Bowers, Alvin Joslin, Frank Aiken,—
    they all
Earned their titles to fame in Corinthian Hall.

But Time, as begrudging the glory that fell
On the spot I revere and remember so well,
Spent his spite on the timbers, the plaster,
    and paint,
And breathed on them all his morbiferous
    taint;

So the trappings of gold and the gear mani-
 fold
Got gangrened with rust and rheumatic with
 mould,
And we saw dank decay and oblivion fall,
Like vapors of night, on Corinthian Hall.

When the gas is ablaze in the opry at night,
And the music goes floating on billows of
 light,
Why, I often regret that I 'm grown to a
 man,
And I pine to be back where my mission
 began,
   And I 'm fain to recall
   Reminiscences all
That come with the thought of Corinthian
 Hall,—
To hear and to see what delighted me then,
And to revel in raptures of boyhood again.

Though Corinthian Hall is a tumble-down
 place,
Which some finical folks have pronounced
 a disgrace,

There is one young old boy, quite as worthy
    as they,
Who, aweary of art as expounded to-day,
        Would surrender what gold
        He 's amassed to behold
A tithe of the wonderful doings of old,
A glimpse of the glories that used to enthrall
Our *crême de la crême* in Corinthian Hall.

THE RED, RED WEST

I 'VE travelled in heaps of countries, and
    studied all kinds of art,
Till there is n't a critic or connoisseur who 's
    properly deemed so smart;
And I 'm free to say that the grand results
    of my explorations show
That somehow paint gets redder the far-
    ther out West I go.

I 've sipped the voluptuous sherbet that the
    Orientals serve,
And I 've felt the glow of red Bordeaux
    tingling each separate nerve;
I 've sampled your classic Massic under an
    arbor green,
And I 've reeked with song a whole night
    long over a brown poteen.

The stalwart brew of the land o' cakes, the
    schnapps of the frugal Dutch,
The much-praised wine of the distant Rhine,
    and the beer praised overmuch,
The ale of dear old London, and the port of
    Southern climes,—
All, *ad infin.*, have I taken in a hundred
    thousand times.

Yet, as I afore-mentioned, these other charms
    are naught
Compared with the paramount gorgeousness
    with which the West is fraught;
For Art and Nature are just the same in the
    land where the porker grows,
And the paint keeps getting redder the far-
    ther out West one goes.

Our savants have never discovered the rea-
    son why this is so,
And ninety per cent. of the laymen care less
    than the savants know;
It answers every purpose that this is mani-
    fest:
The paint keeps getting redder the farther
    you go out West.

Give me no home 'neath the pale pink dome
    of European skies,
No cot for me by the salmon sea that far to
    the southward lies;
But away out West I would build my nest
    on top of a carmine hill,
Where I can paint, without restraint, crea-
    tion redder still!

THE THREE KINGS OF COLOGNE

FROM out Cologne there came three kings
   To worship Jesus Christ, their King.
To Him they sought fine herbs they brought,
   And many a beauteous golden thing;
They brought their gifts to Bethlehem town,
And in that manger set them down.

Then spake the first king, and he said:
   "O Child, most heavenly, bright, and
      fair!
I bring this crown to Bethlehem town
   For Thee, and only Thee, to wear;
So give a heavenly crown to me
When I shall come at last to Thee!"

The second, then.   "I bring Thee here
   This royal robe, O Child!" he cried;
"Of silk 't is spun, and such an one
   There is not in the world beside;

135

So in the day of doom requite
Me with a heavenly robe of white!"

The third king gave his gift, and quoth:
　"Spikenard and myrrh to Thee I bring,
And with these twain would I most fain
　Anoint the body of my King;
So may their incense sometime rise
To plead for me in yonder skies!"

Thus spake the three kings of Cologne,
　That gave their gifts, and went their way;
And now kneel I in prayer hard by
　The cradle of the Child to-day;
Nor crown, nor robe, nor spice I bring
As offering unto Christ, my King.

Yet have I brought a gift the Child
　May not despise, however small;
For here I lay my heart to-day,
　And it is full of love to all.
Take Thou the poor but loyal thing,
My only tribute, Christ, my King!

IPSWICH

IN Ipswich nights are cool and fair,
   And the voice that comes from the yonder
      sea
Sings to the quaint old mansions there
   Of "the time, the time that used to be;"
And the quaint old mansions rock and groan,
And they seem to say in an undertone,
With half a sigh and with half a moan:
   "It was, but it never again will be."

In Ipswich witches weave at night
   Their magic spells with impish glee;
They shriek and laugh in their demon flight
   From the old Main House to the frightened
      sea.

And ghosts of eld come out to weep
Over the town that is fast asleep;
And they sob and they wail, as on they
    creep:
    " It was, but it never again will be."

In Ipswich riseth Heart-Break Hill
    Over against the calling sea;
And through the nights so deep and chill
    Watcheth a maiden constantly,—
Watcheth alone, nor seems to hear
Over the roar of the waves anear
The pitiful cry of a far-off year:
    " It was, but it never again will be."

In Ipswich once a witch I knew,—
    An artless Saxon witch was she;
By that flaxen hair and those eyes of blue,
    Sweet was the spell she cast on me.
Alas! but the years have wrought me ill,
And the heart that is old and battered and
    chill
Seeketh again on Heart-Break Hill
    What was, but never again can be.

Dear Anna, I would not conjure down
   The ghost that cometh to solace me;
I love to think of old Ipswich town,
   Where somewhat better than friends were
      we;
For with every thought of the dear old place
Cometh again the tender grace
Of a Saxon witch's pretty face,
   As it was, and is, and ever shall be.

BILL'S TENOR AND MY BASS

BILL was short and dapper, while I was
thin and tall;
I had flowin' whiskers, but Bill had none at
all;
  Clothes would never seem to set so nice
  on *me* as *him,*—
  Folks used to laugh, and say I was too
  powerful slim,—
But Bill's clothes fit him like the paper on the
wall;
  And we were the sparkin'est beaus in all
  the place
When Bill sung tenor and I sung bass.

Cyrus Baker's oldest girl was member of the
choir,—

Eyes as black as Kelsey's cat, and cheeks as
    red as fire!
    She had the best sopranner voice I think I
      ever heard,—
    Sung "Coronation," "Burlington," and
      "Chiny" like a bird;
Never done better than with Bill a-standin'
    nigh 'er,
    A-holdin' of her hymn-book so she
      would n't lose the place,
    When Bill sung tenor and I sung bass.

Then there was Prudence Hubbard, so cosey-
    like and fat,—
She sung alto, and wore a pee-wee hat;
    Beaued her around one winter, and, first
      thing I knew,
    One evenin' on the portico I up and called
      her "Prue"!
But, sakes alive! she did n't mind a little
    thing like that;
    On all the works of Providence she set a
      cheerful face
    When Bill was singin' tenor and I was
      singin' bass.

Bill, nevermore we two shall share the fun
we used to then,
Nor know the comfort and the peace we had
together when
We lived in Massachusetts in the good old
courtin' days,
And lifted up our voices in psalms and
hymns of praise.
Oh, how I wisht that I could live them
happy times again!
For life, as we boys knew it, had a sweet,
peculiar grace
When you was singin' tenor and I was
singin' bass.

The music folks have nowadays ain't what
it used to be,
Because there ain't no singers now on earth
like Bill and me.
Why, Lemuel Bangs, who used to go to
Springfield twice a year,
Admitted that for singin' Bill and me had
not a peer
When Bill went soarin' up to A and I dropped
down to D!

The old bull-fiddle Beza Dimmitt played
  war n't in the race
'Longside of Bill's high tenor and my so-
  norious bass.

Bill moved to Californy in the spring of '54,
And we folks that used to know him never
    knew him any more;
  Then Cyrus Baker's oldest girl, she kind o'
    pined a spell,
  And, hankerin' after sympathy, it naterally
    befell
That she married Deacon Pitkin's boy, who
    kep' the general store;
  And so the years, the changeful years, have
    rattled on apace
  Since Bill sung tenor and I sung bass.

As I was settin' by the stove this evenin' after
    tea,
I noticed wife kep' hitchin' close and closer
    up to me;
  And as she patched the gingham frock our
    gran'child wore to-day,
  I heerd her gin a sigh that seemed to come
    from fur away.

143

Could n't help inquirin' what the trouble
    might be;
  "Was thinkin' of the time," says Prue,
    a-breshin' at her face,
  "When Bill sung tenor and you sung
    bass."

FIDUCIT

THREE comrades on the German Rhine,
   Defying care and weather,
Together quaffed the mellow wine,
   And sung their songs together.
What recked they of the griefs of life,
   With wine and song to cheer them?
Though elsewhere trouble might be rife,
   It would not come anear them.

Anon one comrade passed away,
   And presently another,
And yet unto the tryst each day
   Repaired the lonely brother;
And still, as gayly as of old,
   That third one, hero-hearted,
Filled to the brim each cup of gold,
   And called to the departed,—

"O comrades mine! I see ye not,
  Nor hear your kindly greeting,
Yet in this old, familiar spot
  Be still our loving meeting!
Here have I filled each bouting-cup
  With juices red and cheery;
I pray ye drink the portion up,
  And as of old make merry!"

And once before his tear-dimmed eyes,
  All in the haunted gloaming,
He saw two ghostly figures rise,
  And quaff the beakers foaming;
He heard two spirit voices call,
  "Fiducit, jovial brother!"
And so forever from that hall
  Went they with one another.

THE "ST. JO GAZETTE"

WHEN I helped 'em run the local on the
    "St. Jo Gazette,"
I was upon familiar terms with every one I
    met;
For "items" were my stock in trade in that
    my callow time,
Before the muses tempted me to try my hand
    at rhyme,—
        Before I found in verses
        Those soothing, gracious mercies,
Less practical, but much more glorious than
    a well-filled purse is.
A votary of Mammon, I hustled round and
    sweat,
And helped 'em run the local on the "St. Jo
    Gazette."
The labors of the day began at half-past
    eight A. M.,

For the farmers came in early, and I had to
tackle them;
And many a noble bit of news I managed to
acquire
By those discreet attentions which all farm-
er-folk admire,
With my daily commentary
On affairs of farm and dairy,
The tone of which anon with subtle pufferies
I 'd vary,—
Oh, many a peck of apples and of peaches
did I get
When I helped 'em run the local on the " St.
Jo Gazette."

Dramatic news was scarce, but when a min-
strel show was due,
Why, Milton Tootle's opera house was then
my rendezvous;
Judge Grubb would give me points about
the latest legal case,
And Dr. Runcie let me print his sermons
when I 'd space;
Of fevers, fractures, humors,
Contusions, fits, and tumors,

Would Dr. Hall or Dr. Baines confirm or
    nail the rumors;
From Colonel Dawes what railroad news
    there was I used to get,—
When I helped 'em run the local on the
    "St. Jo Gazette."

For "personals" the old Pacific House was
    just the place,—
Pap Abell knew the pedigrees of all the hu-
    man race;
And when he 'd gi'n up all he had, he 'd
    drop a subtle wink,
And lead the way where one might wet one's
    whistle with a drink.
      Those drinks at the Pacific,
      When days were sudorific,
Were what Parisians (pray excuse my
    French!) would call "magnifique;"
And frequently an invitation to a meal I 'd
    get
When I helped 'em run the local on the "St.
    Jo Gazette."

And when in rainy weather news was scarce
    as well as slow,

149

To Saxton's bank or Hopkins' store for items
    would I go.
The jokes which Colonel Saxton told were
    old, but good enough
For local application in lieu of better stuff;
       And when the ducks were flying,
       Or the fishing well worth trying—
Gosh! but those "sports" at Hopkins' store
    could beat the world at lying!
And I—I printed all their yarns, though not
    without regret,
When I helped 'em run the local on the
    "St. Jo Gazette."

For squibs political I 'd go to Colonel Waller
    Young,
Or Colonel James N. Burnes, the "statesman
    with the silver tongue;"
Should some old pioneer take sick and die,
    why, then I 'd call
On Frank M. Posegate for the "life," and
    Posegate knew 'em all.
       Lon Tullar used to pony
       Up descriptions that were tony
Of toilets worn at party, ball, or conversa-
    zione;

For the ladies were addicted to the style
    called " deckolett "
When I helped 'em run the local on the " St.
    Jo Gazette."

So was I wont my daily round of labor to
    pursue;
And when came night I found that there
    was still more work to do,—
The telegraph to edit, yards and yards of
    proof to read,
And reprint to be gathered to supply the
    printers' greed.
       Oh, but it takes agility,
       Combined with versatility,
To run a country daily with appropriate
    ability!
There never were a smarter lot of editors,
    I 'll bet,
Than we who whooped up local on the " St.
    Jo Gazette."

Yes, maybe it was irksome; may be a dis-
    content
Rebellious rose amid the toil I daily under-
    went.

151

If so, I don't remember; this only do I
    know,—
My thoughts turn ever fondly to that time
    in old St. Jo.
        The years that speed so fleetly
        Have blotted out completely
All else than that which still remains to solace
    me so sweetly;
The friendships of that time,— ah, me! they
    are as precious yet
As when I was a local on the "St. Jo Ga-
    zette."

IN AMSTERDAM

MEYNHEER Hans Von Der Bloom has got
    A majazin in Kalverstraat,
Where one may buy for sordid gold
Wares quaint and curious, new and old.
Here are antiquities galore,—
The jewels which Dutch monarchs wore,
Swords, teacups, helmets, platters, clocks,
Bright Dresden jars, dull Holland crocks,
And all those joys I might rehearse
That please the eye, but wreck the purse.

I most admired an ancient bed,
With ornate carvings at its head,—
A massive frame of dingy oak,
Whose curious size and mould bespoke
Prodigious age. "How much?" I cried.
"Ein tousand gildens," Hans replied;

And then the honest Dutchman said
A king once owned that glorious bed,—
King Fritz der Foorst, of blessed fame,
Had owned and slept within the same!

Then long I stood and mutely gazed,
By reminiscent splendors dazed,
And I had bought it right away,
Had I the wherewithal to pay.
But, lacking of the needed pelf,
I thus discoursed within myself:
"O happy Holland! where 's the bliss
That can approximate to this
Possession of the rare antique
Which maniacs hanker for and seek?
My native land is full of stuff
That 's good, but is not old enough.
Alas! it has no oaken beds
Wherein have slumbered royal heads,
No relic on whose face we see
The proof of grand antiquity."

Thus reasoned I a goodly spell
Until, perchance, my vision fell
Upon a trademark at the head
Of Fritz der Foorst's old oaken bed,—

A rampant wolverine, and round
This strange device these words I found:
"Patent Antique.   Birkey & Gay,
Grand Rapids, Michigan, U. S. A."

At present I 'm not saying much
About the simple, guileless Dutch;
And as it were a loathsome spot
I keep away from Kalverstraat,
Determined when I want a bed
In which hath slept a royal head
I 'll patronize no middleman,
But deal direct with Michigan.

TO THE PASSING SAINT

AS to-night you came your way,
  Bearing earthward heavenly joy,
Tell me, O dear saint, I pray,
  Did you see my little boy?

By some fairer voice beguiled,
  Once he wandered from my sight;
He is such a little child,
  He should have my love this night.

It has been so many a year,—
  Oh, so many a year since then!
Yet he was so very dear,
  Surely he will come again.

If upon your way you see
  One whose beauty is divine,
Will you send him back to me?
  He is lost, and he is mine.

Tell him that his little chair
  Nestles where the sunbeams meet,
That the shoes he used to wear
  Yearn to kiss his dimpled feet.

Tell him of each pretty toy
  That was wont to share his glee;
Maybe that will bring my boy
  Back to them and back to me.

O dear saint, as on you go
  Through the glad and sparkling frost,
Bid those bells ring high and low
  For a little child that 's lost!

O dear saint, that blessest men
  With the grace of Christmas joy,
Soothe this heart with love again,—
  Give me back my little boy!

THE FISHERMAN'S FEAST

OF all the gracious gifts of Spring,
  Is there another can surpass
This delicate, voluptuous thing,—
    This dapple-green, plump-shouldered
      bass?
Upon a damask napkin laid,
  What exhalations superfine
Our gustatory nerves pervade,
    Provoking quenchless thirsts for wine!

The ancients loved this noble fish;
  And, coming from the kitchen fire
All piping hot upon a dish,
  What raptures did he not inspire?
"Fish should swim twice," they used to
    say,—
  Once in their native, vapid brine,
And then again, a better way —
    You understand; fetch on the wine!

Ah, dainty monarch of the flood,
  How often have I cast for you,
How often sadly seen you scud
  Where weeds and water-lilies grew!
How often have you filched my bait,
  How often snapped my treacherous line!
Yet here I have you on this plate,—
  You *shall* swim twice, and *now* in *wine*.

And harkee, garçon! let the blood
  Of cobwebbed years be spilled for him,—
Ay, in a rich Burgundian flood
  This piscatorial pride should swim;
So, were he living, he would say
  He gladly died for me and mine,
And, as it were his native spray,
  He 'd lash the sauce — what, ho! the
    wine!

I would it were ordained for me
  To share your fate, O finny friend!
I surely were not loath to be
  Reserved for such a noble end;
For when old Chronos, gaunt and grim,
  At last reels in his ruthless line,
What were my ecstasy to swim
  In wine, in wine, in glorious wine!

Well, here 's a health to you, sweet Spring!
   And, prithee, whilst I stick to earth,
Come hither every year and bring
   The boons provocative of mirth;
And should your stock of bass run low,
   However much I might repine,
I think I might survive the blow,
   If plied with wine and still more wine!

THE ONION TART

O F tarts there be a thousand kinds,
    So versatile the art,
And, as we all have different minds,
    Each has his favorite tart;
But those which most delight the rest
    Methinks should suit me not:
The onion tart doth please me best,—
    Ach, Gott! mein lieber Gott!

Where but in Deutschland can be found
    This boon of which I sing?
Who but a Teuton could compound
    This *sui generis* thing?
None with the German frau can vie
    In arts cuisine, I wot,
Whose *summum bonum* breeds the sigh,
    "Ach, Gott! mein lieber Gott!"

You slice the fruit upon the dough,
   And season to the taste,
Then in an oven (not too slow)
   The viand should be placed;
And when 't is done, upon a plate
   You serve it piping hot,
Your nostrils and your eyes dilate,—
   Ach, Gott! mein lieber Gott!

It sweeps upon the sight and smell
   In overwhelming tide,
And then the sense of taste as well
   Betimes is gratified:
Three noble senses drowned in bliss!
   I prithee tell me, what
Is there beside compares with this?
   Ach, Gott! mein lieber Gott!

For if the fruit be proper young,
   And if the crust be good,
How shall they melt upon the tongue
   Into a savory flood!
How seek the Mecca down below,
   And linger round that spot,
Entailing weeks and months of woe,—
   Ach, Gott! mein lieber Gott!

If Nature gives men appetites
    For things that won't digest,
Why, let *them* eat whatso delights,
    And let *her* stand the rest;
And though the sin involve the cost
    Of Carlsbad, like as not
'T is better to have loved and lost,—
    Ach, Gott! mein lieber Gott!

Beyond the vast, the billowy tide,
    Where my compatriots dwell,
All kinds of victuals have I tried,
    All kinds of drinks, as well;
But nothing known to Yankee art
    Appears to reach *the spot*
Like this Teutonic onion tart,—
    Ach, Gott! mein lieber Gott!

So, though I quaff of Carlsbad's tide
    As full as I can hold,
And for complete reform inside
    Plank down my hoard of gold,
Remorse shall not consume my heart,
    Nor sorrow vex my lot,
For I have eaten onion tart,—
    Ach, Gott! mein lieber Gott!

GRANDMA'S BOMBAZINE

IT 's everywhere that women fair invite
  and please my eye,
And that on dress I lay much stress I can't
  and sha' n't deny:
The English dame who 's all aflame with
  divers colors bright,
The Teuton belle, the ma'moiselle,— all give
  me keen delight;
And yet I 'll say, go where I may, I never
  yet have seen
A dress that 's quite as grand a sight as was
  that bombazine.

Now, you must know 't was years ago this
  quaint but noble gown
Flashed in one day, the usual way, upon our
  solemn town.

'T was Fisk who sold for sordid gold that
    gravely scrumptious thing,—
Jim Fisk, the man who drove a span that
    would have joyed a king,—
And grandma's eye fell with a sigh upon
    that sombre sheen,
And grandpa's purse looked much the worse
    for grandma's bombazine.

Though ten years old, I never told the neigh-
    bors of the gown;
For grandma said, "This secret, Ned, must
    not be breathed in town."
The sitting-room for days of gloom was in a
    dreadful mess
When that quaint dame, Miss Kelsey, came
    to make the wondrous dress:
To fit and baste and stitch a waist, with
    whalebones in between,
Is precious slow, as all folks know who 've
    made a bombazine.

With fortitude dear grandma stood the trial
    to the end
(The nerve we find in womankind I cannot
    comprehend!);

And when 't was done, resolved that none
 should guess at the surprise,
Within the press she hid that dress, secure
 from prying eyes;
For grandma knew a thing or two,— by
 which remark I mean
That Sundays were the days for her to wear
 that bombazine.

I need not state she got there late; and, sail-
 ing up the aisle
With regal grace, on grandma's face reposed
 a conscious smile.
It fitted so, above, below, and hung so well
 all round,
That there was not one faulty spot a critic
 could have found.
How proud I was of her, because she looked
 so like a queen!
And that was why, perhaps, that I admired
 the bombazine.

But there *were* those, as you 'd suppose,
 who scorned that perfect gown;
For ugly-grained old cats obtained in that
 New England town:

The Widow White spat out her spite in one:
    "It does n't fit!"
The Packard girls (they wore false curls) all
    giggled like to split;
Sophronia Wade, the sour old maid, *she*
    turned a bilious green,
When she descried that joy and pride, my
    grandma's bombazine.

But grandma knew, and I did, too, that gown
    was wondrous fine, —
The envious sneers and jaundiced jeers were
    a conclusive sign.
Why, grandpa said it went ahead of all the
    girls in town,
And, saying this, he snatched a kiss that
    like to burst that gown;
But, blushing red, my grandma said, "Oh,
    is n't grandpa mean!"
Yet evermore my grandma wore *his* favorite
    bombazine.

And when she died that sombre pride passed
    down to heedless heirs, —
Alas, the day 't was hung away beneath the
    kitchen stairs!

Thence in due time, with dust and grime,
    came foes on foot and wing,
And made their nests and sped their guests
    in that once beauteous thing.
'T is so, forsooth! Time's envious tooth
    corrodes each human scene;
And so, at last, to ruin passed my grandma's
    bombazine.

Yet to this day, I 'm proud to say, it plays
    a grateful part, —
The thoughts it brings are of such things as
    touch and warm my heart.
This gown, my dear, you show me here I 'll
    own is passing fair,
Though I 'll confess it 's no such dress as
    grandma used to wear.
Yet wear it, *do;* perchance when you and I
    are off the scene,
Our boy shall sing *this* comely thing as *I* the
    bombazine.

RARE ROAST BEEF

WHEN the numerous distempers to
    which all flesh is heir
Torment us till our very souls are reeking
    with despair;
When that monster fiend, Dyspepsy, rears
    its spectral hydra head,
Filling *bon vivants* and epicures with certain
    nameless dread;
When *any* ill of body or of intellect abounds,
Be it sickness known to Galen or disease un-
    known to Lowndes,—
In such a dire emergency it is my firm belief
That there is no diet quite so good as rare
    roast beef.

And even when the body 's in the very
    prime of health,
When sweet contentment spreads upon the
    cheeks her rosy wealth,
And when a man devours three meals per
    day and pines for more,
And growls because instead of three square
    meals there are not four,—
Well, even then, though cake and pie do
    service on the side,
And coffee is a luxury that may not be
    denied,
Still of the many viands there is one that 's
    hailed as chief,
And that, as you are well aware, is rare
    roast beef.

Some like the sirloin, but I think the porter-
    house is best,—
'T is juicier and tenderer and meatier than
    the rest;
Put on this roast a dash of salt, and then of
    water pour
Into the sizzling dripping-pan a cupful, and
    no more;

The oven being hot, the roast will cook in
    half an hour;
Then to the juices in the pan you add a little
    flour,
And so you get a gravy that is called the cap
    sheaf
Of that glorious *summum bonum,* rare roast
    beef.

Served on a platter that is hot, and carved
    with thin, keen knife,
How does this savory viand enhance the
    worth of life!
Give me no thin and shadowy slice, but a
    thick and steaming slab,—
Who would not choose a generous hunk to
    a bloodless little dab?
Upon a nice hot plate how does the juicy
    morceau steam,
A symphony in scarlet or a red incarnate
    dream!
Take from me eyes and ears and all, O Time,
    thou ruthless thief!
Except these teeth wherewith to deal with
    rare roast beef.

Most every kind and rôle of modern victuals
    have I tried,
Including roasted, fricasseed, broiled, toasted,
    stewed, and fried,
Your canvasbacks and papa-bottes and mut-
    ton-chops subese,
Your patties *à la* Turkey and your dough-
    nuts *à la* grease;
I've whirled away dyspeptic hours with crabs
    in marble halls,
And in the lowly cottage I've experienced
    codfish balls;
But I've never found a viand that could so
    allay all grief
And soothe the cockles of the heart as rare
    roast beef.

I honor that sagacious king who, in a grate-
    ful mood,
Knighted the savory loin that on the royal
    table stood;
And as for me I'd ask no better friend than
    this good roast,
Which is my squeamish stomach's fortress
    (*feste Burg*) and host;

For with this ally with me I can mock Dyspepsy's wrath,
Can I pursue the joy of Wisdom's pleasant,
  peaceful path.
So I do off my vest and let my waistband out
  a reef
When I soever set me down to rare roast
  beef.

OLD TIMES, OLD FRIENDS, OLD LOVE

THERE are no days like the good old
  days,—
  The days when we were youthful!
When humankind were pure of mind,
  And speech and deeds were truthful;
Before a love for sordid gold
  Became man's ruling passion,
And before each dame and maid became
  Slave to the tyrant fashion!

There are no girls like the good old girls,—
  Against the world I 'd stake 'em!
As buxom and smart and clean of heart
  As the Lord knew how to make 'em!
They were rich in spirit and common-sense,
  And piety all supportin';
They could bake and brew, and had taught
    school, too,
And they made such likely courtin'!

There are no boys like the good old boys,—
   When *we* were boys together!
When the grass was sweet to the brown
     bare feet
   That dimpled the laughing heather;
When the pewee sung to the summer dawn
   Of the bee in the billowy clover,
Or down by the mill the whip-poor-will
   Echoed his night song over.

There is no love like the good old love,—
   The love that mother gave us!
We are old, old men, yet we pine again
   For that precious grace,—God save us!
So we dream and dream of the good old times,
   And our hearts grow tenderer, fonder,
As those dear old dreams bring soothing
     gleams
   Of heaven away off yonder.

BION'S SONG OF EROS

EROS is the god of love;
  He and I are hand-in-glove.
  All the gentle, gracious Muses
    Follow Eros where he leads,
  And they bless the bard who chooses
    To proclaim love's famous deeds;
Him they serve in rapturous glee,—
That is why they 're good to me.

Sometimes I have gone astray
From love's sunny, flowery way:
  How I floundered, how I stuttered!
    And, deprived of ways and means,
  What egregious rot I uttered,—
    Such as suits the magazines!
I was rescued only when
Eros called me back again.

Gods forefend that I should shun
That benignant Mother's son!
  Why, the poet who refuses
    To emblazon love's delights
  Gets the mitten from the Muses,—
    Then what balderdash he writes!
I love Love; which being so,
See how smooth my verses flow!

Gentle Eros, lead the way,—
I will follow while I may:
  Be thy path by hill or hollow,
    I will follow fast and free;
  And when I 'm too old to follow,
    I will sit and sing of thee,—
Potent still in intellect,
Sit, and sing, and retrospect.

MR. BILLINGS OF LOUISVILLE

THERE are times in one's life which one
   cannot forget;
And the time I remember 's the evening I
   met
A haughty young scion of bluegrass renown
Who made my acquaintance while painting
   the town:
A handshake, a cocktail, a smoker, and then
Mr. Billings of Louisville touched me for ten.

There flowed in his veins the blue blood of
   the South,
And a cynical smile curled his sensuous
   mouth;
He quoted from Lanier and Poe by the yard,
But his purse had been hit by the war, and
   hit hard:
I felt that he honored and flattered me when
Mr. Billings of Louisville touched me for ten.

I wonder that never again since that night
A vision of Billings has hallowed my sight;
I pine for the sound of his voice and the thrill
That comes with the touch of a ten-dollar
    bill:
I wonder and pine; for — I say it again —
Mr. Billings of Louisville touched me for ten.

I 've heard what old Whittier sung of Miss
    Maud;
But all such philosophy 's nothing but fraud;
To one who 's a bear in Chicago to-day,
With wheat going up, and the devil to pay,
These words are the saddest of tongue or of
    pen:
"Mr. Billings of Louisville touched me for
    ten."

POET AND KING

THOUGH I am king, I have no throne
    Save this rough wooden siege alone;
I have no empire, yet my sway
Extends a myriad leagues away;
No servile vassal bends his knee
In grovelling reverence to me,
Yet at my word all hearts beat high,
And there is fire in every eye,
And love and gratitude they bring
As tribute unto me, a king.

The folk that throng the busy street
Know not it is a king they meet;
And I am glad there is not seen
The monarch in my face and mien.
I should not choose to be the cause
Of fawning or of coarse applause:
I am content to know the arts
Wherewith to lord it o'er their hearts;
For when unto their hearts I sing,
I am a king, I am a king!

My sceptre,— see, it is a pen!
Wherewith I rule these hearts of men.
Sometime it pleaseth to beguile
Its monarch fancy with a smile;
Sometime it is athirst for tears:
And so adown the laurelled years
I walk, the noblest lord on earth,
Dispensing sympathy and mirth.
Aha! it is a magic thing
That makes me what I am,— a king!

Let empires crumble as they may,
Proudly I hold imperial sway;
The sunshine and the rain of years
Are human smiles and human tears
That come or vanish at my call,—
I am the monarch of them all!
Mindful alone of this am I:
The songs I sing shall never die;
Not even envious Death can wring
His glory from so great a king.

Come, brother, be a king with me,
And rule mankind eternally;
Lift up the weak, and cheer the strong,
Defend the truth, combat the wrong!

You 'll find no sceptre like the pen
To hold and sway the hearts of men;
Its edicts flow in blood and tears
That will outwash the flood of years:
So, brother, sing your songs, oh, sing!
And be with me a king, a king!

LYDIA DICK

WHEN I was a boy at college,
  Filling up with classic knowledge,
Frequently I wondered why
Old Professor Demas Bentley
Used to praise so eloquently
  "Opera Horatii."

Toiling on a season longer
Till my reasoning powers got stronger,
  As my observation grew,
I became convinced that mellow,
Massic-loving poet fellow,
  Horace, knew a thing or two.

Yes, we sophomores figured duly
That, if we appraised him truly,
  Horace must have been a brick;
And no wonder that with ranting
Rhymes he went a-gallivanting
  Round with sprightly Lydia Dick!

183

For that pink of female gender
Tall and shapely was, and slender,
  Plump of neck and bust and arms;
While the raiment that invested
Her so jealously suggested
  Certain more potential charms.

Those dark eyes of hers that fired him,
Those sweet accents that inspired him,
  And her crown of glorious hair,—
These things baffle my description:
I should have a fit conniption
  If I tried; so I forbear.

Maybe Lydia had her betters;
Anyway, this man of letters
  Took that charmer as his pick.
Glad — yes, glad I am to know it!
I, a *fin de siècle* poet,
  Sympathize with Lydia Dick!

Often in my arbor shady
I fall thinking of that lady,
  And the pranks she used to play;
And I 'm cheered,— for all we sages
Joy when from those distant ages
  Lydia dances down our way.

Otherwise some folks might wonder,
With good reason, why in thunder
   Learned professors, dry and prim,
Find such solace in the giddy
Pranks that Horace played with Liddy
   Or that Liddy played on him.

Still this world of ours rejoices
In those ancient singing voices,
   And our hearts beat high and quick,
To the cadence of old Tiber
Murmuring praise of roistering Liber
   And of charming Lydia Dick.

Still Digentia, downward flowing,
Prattleth to the roses blowing
   By the dark, deserted grot.
Still Soracte, looming lonely,
Watcheth for the coming only
   Of a ghost that cometh not.

LIZZIE

I WONDER ef all wimmin air
   Like Lizzie is when we go out
To theatres an' concerts where
   Is things the papers talk about.
Do other wimmin fret an' stew
   Like they wuz bein' crucified,—
Frettin' a show or concert through,
   With wonderin' ef the baby cried?

Now Lizzie knows that gran'ma 's there
   To see that everything is right;
Yet Lizzie thinks that gran'ma's care
   Ain't good enuff f'r baby, quite.
Yet what am I to answer when
   She kind uv fidgets at my side,
An' asks me every now an' then,
   "I wonder ef the baby cried"?

Seems like she seen two little eyes
    A-pinin' f'r their mother's smile;
Seems like she heern the pleadin' cries
    Uv one she thinks uv all the while;
An' so she 's sorry that she come.
    An' though she allus tries to hide
The truth, she 'd ruther stay to hum
    Than wonder ef the baby cried.

Yes, wimmin folks is all alike —
    By Lizzie you kin jedge the rest;
There never wuz a little tyke,
    But that his mother loved him best.
And nex' to bein' what I be —
    The husband uv my gentle bride —
I 'd wisht I wuz that croodlin' wee,
    With Lizzie wonderin' ef I cried.

ALWAYS RIGHT

DON'T take on so, Hiram,
  But do what you 're told to do;
It 's fair to suppose that yer mother knows
  A heap sight more than you.
I 'll allow that sometimes *her* way
  Don't seem the wisest, quite;
But the *easiest* way,
When she 's had her say,
  Is to reckon yer mother is right.

Courted her ten long winters,
  Saw her to singin'-school;
When she went down one spell to town,
  I cried like a durned ol' fool;
Got mad at the boys for callin'
  When I sparked her Sunday night:
But she said she knew
A thing or two,—
  An' I reckoned yer mother wuz right.

I courted till I wuz aging,
   And she wuz past her prime,—
I'd have died, I guess, if she had n't said yes
   When I popped f'r the hundredth time.
Said she 'd never have took me
   If I had n't stuck so tight;
Opined that we
Could never agree,—
   And I reckon yer mother wuz right!

"TROT, MY GOOD STEED, TROT!"

WHERE my true love abideth
    I make my way to-night;
    Lo! waiting, she
    Espieth me,
And calleth in delight:
"I see his steed anear
Come trotting with my dear,—
Oh, idle not, good steed, but trot,
    Trot thou my lover here!"

Aloose I cast the bridle,
    And ply the whip and spur;
    And gayly I
    Speed this reply,
While faring on to her:
"Oh, true love, fear thou not!
I seek our trysting spot;
And double feed be yours, my steed,
    If you more swiftly trot."

I vault from out the saddle,
  And make my good steed fast;
    Then to my breast
    My love is pressed,—
  At last, true heart, at last!
  The garden drowsing lies,
  The stars fold down their eyes,—
In this dear spot, my steed, neigh not,
  Nor stamp in restless wise!

O passing sweet communion
  Of young hearts, warm and true!
    To thee belongs
    The old, old songs
  Love finds forever new.
  We sing those songs, and then
  Cometh the moment when
It's, "Good steed, trot from this dear spot,—
  Trot, trot me home again!"

PROVIDENCE AND THE DOG

WHEN I was young and callow, which
    was many years ago,
Within me the afflatus went surging to and
    fro;
And so I wrote a tragedy that fairly reeked
    with gore,
With every act concluding with the dead
    piled on the floor,—
A mighty effort, by the gods! and after I had
    read
The manuscript to Daly, that dramatic cen-
    sor said:
" The plot is most exciting, and I like the
    dialogue;
You should take the thing to Providence, and
    try it on a dog."

McCambridge organized a troupe, including
    many a name
Unknown alike to guileless me, to riches, and
    to fame.
A pompous man whose name was Rae was
    Nestor of this troupe,—
Amphibious, he was quite at home outside
    or in the soup!
The way McCambridge billed him! Why,
    such dreams in red and green
Had ne'er before upon the boards of Yan-
    keedom been seen;
And my proud name was heralded,— oh,
    that I'd gone incog.,
When we took that play to Providence to
    try it on a dog!

Shall I forget the awful day we struck that
    wretched town?
Yet in what melting irony the treacherous
    sun beamed down!
The sale of seats had not been large; but
    then McCambridge said
The factory people seldom bought their
    seats so far ahead,

And Rae indorsed McCambridge.   So they
     partly set at rest
The natural misgivings that perturbed my
     youthful breast;
For I wondered and lamented that the town
     was not agog
When I took my play to Providence to try
     it on a dog.

They never came at all,— aha! I knew it all
     the time,—
They never came to see and hear my tragedy
     sublime.
Oh, fateful moment when the curtain rose
     on act the first!
Oh, moment fateful to the soul for wealth
     and fame athirst!
But lucky factory girls and boys to stay away
     that night,
When the author's fervid soul was touched
     by disappointment's blight,—
When desolation settled down on me like
     some dense fog
For having tempted Providence, and tried it
     on a dog!

194

Those actors did n't know their parts; they
    maundered to and fro,
Ejaculating platitudes that were quite *mal à
    propos;*
And when I sought to reprimand the grace-
    less scamps, the lot
Turned fiercely on me, and denounced my
    charming play as rot.
I might have stood their bitter taunts with-
    out a passing grunt,
If I 'd had a word of solace from the people
    out in front;
But that chilly corporal's guard sat round like
    bumps upon a log
When I played that play at Providence with
    designs upon the dog.

We went with lots of baggage, but we did
    n't bring it back,—
For who would be so hampered as he walks
    a railway track?
"Oh, ruthless muse of tragedy! what prodi-
    gies of shame,
What marvels of injustice are committed in
    thy name!"

Thus groaned I in the spirit, as I strode what
    stretch of ties
'Twixt Providence, Rhode Island, and my
    native Gotham lies;
But Rae, McCambridge, and the rest kept
    up a steady jog,—
'T was not the first time they had plied their
    arts upon the dog.

So much for my first battle with the fickle
    goddess, Fame,—
And I hear that some folks nowadays are
    faring just the same.
Oh, hapless he that on the graceless Yankee
    dog relies!
The dog fares stout and hearty, and the play
    it is that dies.
So ye with tragedies to try, I beg of you,
    beware!
Put not your trust in Providence, that most
    delusive snare;
Cast, if you will, your pearls of thought be-
    fore the Western hog,
But never go to Providence to try it on a
    dog.

GETTIN' ON

WHEN I wuz somewhat younger,
   I wuz reckoned purty gay;
I had my fling at everything
   In a rollickin', coltish way.
But times have strangely altered
   Since sixty years ago —
This age of steam an' things don't seem
   Like the age I used to know.
Your modern innovations
   Don't suit me, I confess,
As did the ways of the good ol' days,—
   But I 'm gettin' on, I guess.

I set on the piazza,
   An' hitch round with the sun;
Sometimes, mayhap, I take a nap,
   Waitin' till school is done.
An' then I tell the children

The things I done in youth,—
An' near as I can, as a vener'ble man,
    I stick to the honest truth,—
But the looks of them 'at listen
    Seem sometimes to express
The remote idee that I 'm gone—you see?—
    An' I *am* gettin' on, I guess.

I get up in the mornin',
    An', nothin' else to do,
Before the rest are up an' dressed,
    I read the papers through.
I hang round with the women
    All day an' hear 'em talk;
An' while they sew or knit I show
    The baby how to walk.
An', somehow, I feel sorry
    When they put away his dress
An' cut his curls ('cause they 're like a
        girl's!)—
    I 'm gettin' on, I guess.

Sometimes, with twilight round me,
    I see, or seem to see,
A distant shore where friends of yore
    Linger an' watch for me.

Sometimes I 've heered 'em callin'
    So tender-like 'nd low
That it almost seemed like a dream I dreamed,
    Or an echo of long ago;
An' sometimes on my forehead
    There falls a soft caress,
Or the touch of a hand,— you understand,—
    I 'm gettin' on, I guess.

THE SCHNELLEST ZUG

FROM Hanover to Leipzig is but a little
    way,
Yet the journey by the so-called schnellest
    zug consumes a day;
You start at half-past ten or so, and not till
    nearly night
Do the double towers of Magdeburg loom
    up before your sight;
From thence to Leipzig 's quick enough,—
    of that I 'll not complain,—
But from Hanover to Magdeburg — confound
    that schnellest train!

The Germans say that " schnell " means fast,
    and " schnellest " faster yet,—
In all my life no grimmer bit of humor have
    I met!

Why, thirteen miles an hour 's the greatest
    speed they ever go,
While on the engine piston-rods do moss
    and lichens grow;
And yet the average Teuton will presumptu-
    ously maintain
That one *can't* know what swiftness is till
    he 's tried das schnellest train!

Fool that I was! I should have walked,—
    I had no time to waste;
The little journey I had planned I had to do
    in haste,—
The quaint old town of Leipzig with its lit-
    erary mart,
And Dresden with its crockery-shops and
    wondrous wealth of art,
The Saxon Alps, the Carlsbad cure for all
    dyspeptic pain,—
These were the ends I had in view when I
    took that schnellest train.

The natives dozed around me, yet none too
    deep to hear
The guard's sporadic shout of "funf minu-
    ten" (meaning beer);

I counted forty times at least that voice an-
nounce the stops
Required of those fat natives to glut their
greed for hops,
Whilst *I* crouched in a corner, a monument
to woe,
And thought unholy, awful things, and felt
my whiskers grow!

And then, the wretched sights one sees
while travelling by that train,—
The women doing men-folks' work at har-
vesting the grain,
Or sometimes grubbing in the soil, or hitched
to heavy carts
Beside the family cow or dog, doing their
slavish parts!
The husbands strut in soldier garb,—indeed
they were too vain
To let creation see *them* work from that
creeping schnellest train!

I found the German language all too feeble
to convey
The sentiments that surged through my dyspeptic hulk that day;

202

I had recourse to English, and exploded
without stint
Such virile Anglo-Saxon as would never do
in print,
But which assuaged my rising gorge and
cooled my seething brain
While snailing on to Magdeburg upon that
schnellest train.

The typical New England freight that maun-
ders to and fro,
The upper Mississippi boats, the bumptious
B. & O.,
The creeping Southern railroads with their
other creeping things,
The Philadelphy cable that is run out West
for rings,
The Piccadilly 'buses with their constant roll
and shake,—
All have I tried, and yet I 'd give the
"schnellest zug" the cake!

My countrymen, if ever you should seek the
German clime,
Put not your trust in Baedeker if you are
pressed for time;

From Hanover to Magdeburg is many a
    weary mile
By "schnellest zug," but done afoot it seems
    a tiny while;
Walk, swim, or skate, and then the task will
    not appear in vain,
But you'll break the third commandment if
    you take the schnellest train!

BETHLEHEM-TOWN

AS I was going to Bethlehem-town,
Upon the earth I cast me down
All underneath a little tree
That whispered in this wise to me:
"Oh, I shall stand on Calvary
And bear what burthen saveth thee!"

As up I fared to Bethlehem-town,
I met a shepherd coming down,
And thus he quoth: "A wondrous sight
Hath spread before mine eyes this night,—
An angel host most fair to see,
That sung full sweetly of a tree
That shall uplift on Calvary
What burthen saveth you and me!"

And as I gat to Bethlehem-town,
Lo! wise men came that bore a crown.
"Is there," cried I, "in Bethlehem
A King shall wear this diadem?"
"Good sooth," they quoth, "and it is He
That shall be lifted on the tree
And freely shed on Calvary
What blood redeemeth us and thee!"

Unto a Child in Bethlehem-town
The wise men came and brought the crown;
And while the infant smiling slept,
Upon their knees they fell and wept;
But, with her babe upon her knee,
Naught recked that Mother of the tree,
That should uplift on Calvary
What burthen saveth all and me.

Again I walk in Bethlehem-town
And think on Him that wears the crown.
I may not kiss His feet again,
Nor worship Him as did I then;
My King hath died upon the tree,
And hath outpoured on Calvary
What blood redeemeth you and me!

THE DOINGS OF DELSARTE

IN former times my numerous rhymes ex-
cited general mirth,
And I was then of all good men the merriest
man on earth;
And my career
From year to year
Was full of cheer
And things,
Despite a few regrets, perdieu! which grim
dyspepsia brings;
But now how strange and harsh a change
has come upon the scene!
Horrors appall the life where all was formerly
so serene:
Yes, wasting care hath cast its snare about
my honest heart,
Because, alas! it hath come to pass my
daughter 's learned Delsarte.

In flesh and joint and every point the coun-
     terpart of me,
She grew so fast she grew at last a marvel-
     ous thing to see, —
Long, gaunt, and slim, each gangling limb
     played stumbling-block to t' other,
The which excess of awkwardness quite
     mortified her mother.
Now, as for me, I like to see the carriages
     uncouth
Which certify to all the shy, unconscious
     age of youth.
If maidenkind be pure of mind, industrious,
     tidy, smart,
What need that they should fool away their
     youth upon Delsarte ?

In good old times my numerous rhymes
     occasioned general mirth,
But now you see
       Revealed in me
          The gloomiest bard on earth.
I sing no more of the joys of yore that
     marked my happy life,
But rather those depressing woes with which
     the present 's rife.

Unreconciled to that gaunt child, who 's now
    a fashion-plate,
One song I raise in Art's dispraise, and so do
    I fight with Fate:
This gangling bard has found it hard to see
    his counterpart
Long, loose, and slim, divorced from him by
    that hectic dude, Delsarte.

      Where'er she goes,
      She loves to pose,
    In classic attitudes,
And droop her eyes in languid wise, and
    feign abstracted moods;
      And she, my child,
      Who all so wild,
    So helpless and so sweet,
That once she knew not what to do with
    those great big hands and feet,
Now comes and goes with such repose, so
    calmly sits or stands,
Is so discreet with both her feet, so deft with
    both her hands.
Why, when I see that satire on me, I give
    an angry start,

And I utter one word — it is commonly
    heard — derogatory to Delsarte.

In years gone by 't was said that I was quite
    a scrumptious man;
Conceit galore had I before this Delsarte
    craze began;
But now these wise
        Folks criticise
             My figure and my face,
And I opine they even incline to sneer at my
    musical bass.
Why, sometimes they presume to say this
    wart upon my cheek
Is not refined, and remarks unkind they pass
    on that antique.
With lusty bass and charms of face and fig-
    ure will I part
Ere they extort this grand old wart to placate
    their Delsarte.

Oh, wretched day! as all shall say who 've
    known my Muse before,
When by this rhyme you see that I 'm not
    in it any more.

Good-by the mirth that over earth diffused
    such keen delight;
The old-time bard
        Of pork and lard
            Is plainly out of sight.
All withered now about his brow the laurel
    fillets droop,
While Lachesis brews
        For the poor old Muse
            A portion of scalding soup.
Engrave this line, O friends of mine! over
    my broken heart:
"He hustled and strove, and fancied he
    throve, till his daughter learned Del-
    sarte."